COTSWOLD WALKS

Church gate, Stow-on-the-Wold. (Walk 20)

Cotswold Walks
Book 1: North

by
Clive Holmes

CICERONE PRESS
MILNTHORPE, CUMBRIA

ISBN 1 85284 139 7
A catalogue record for this book is available from the British Library.

DEDICATION

For Malcolm

ACKNOWLEDGEMENTS

The preparation of this series of Cotswolds Walks has been a long process, it has also been a most interesting and enriching one but without the help of others it might not have reached fruition.

I would like to thank my wife for her constructive advice about routes and places of interest, for her administrative help and above all for her company on each of the sixty walks, in all weathers. Further, my thanks are also due to all members of my family and to those friends as well who joined us for some of the walks in the northern region.

Finally I must pay tribute to the surgical team, the nursing staff and to the physiotherapists of Luton and Dunstable Hospital, Bedfordshire, who worked so hard to give me back the use of my damaged fingers of my right-hand shortly after the commencement of this work. I will always be grateful!

Clive Holmes

Front Cover: Stow-on-the-Wold
Photo: Malcolm Holmes

CONTENTS

Old water source and memorial at Ilmington (Walk 1)

Advice to Readers

Readers are advised that whilst every effort is taken by the author to ensure the accuracy of this guidebook, changes can occur which may affect the contents. It is advisable to check locally on transport, accommodation, shops etc but even rights-of-way can be altered and, more especially overseas, paths can be eradicated by landslip, forest fires or changes of ownership.

The publisher would welcome notes of any such changes

INTRODUCTION

The History of the Region

"I praise God and ever shall
It is the sheep hath paid for it all"

So reads the inscription on a Cotswolds merchant's house: an accurate and enlightened summary of the reasons for the Cotswold's development and the survival of the region in its present form, untarnished by industry and characterised by a wealth of beautiful landscapes and settlements rich in history and character. A walkers paradise indeed.

The area that we know today as the Cotswolds became rich over the past generations thanks to sheep farming and in particular to the local breed of sheep known as The Cotswold, each of which, it was said, could produce 28lb of fleece. With the passage of time mills sprang up in the valleys, where the rivers provided power for the manufacture of cloth, thus increasing the wealth of the region.

In the early days the sheep's fleece was exported to Europe to be woven. However, during the reign of Edward III it became apparent that the English would do better to both produce *and* weave the fleece. Flemish weavers were persuaded to emigrate to England, thus the wool industry was founded. From that point on trade rapidly flourished and in time came to dominate the economy.

At its peak the area known as the Cotswolds was producing over half of the total national wool product, so great had become the capacity of the area. Half of the local population were employed in some part of the woollen cloth production process and the area grazed over half a million sheep. The region as a whole was very comfortably off, but it was the merchants and the dealers who profited enormously, so much so that they were able to lend money to the Exchequer and to build fine houses, develop their estates and put vast amounts of money into their local churches.

Unfortunately, this happy state of affairs did not last forever and whilst other parts of Britain were developing and prospering during the industrial revolution, the Cotswolds generally went into a decline. Many of the mills closed and whole villages fell into ruin. Families moved out of the area, the men folk seeking employment

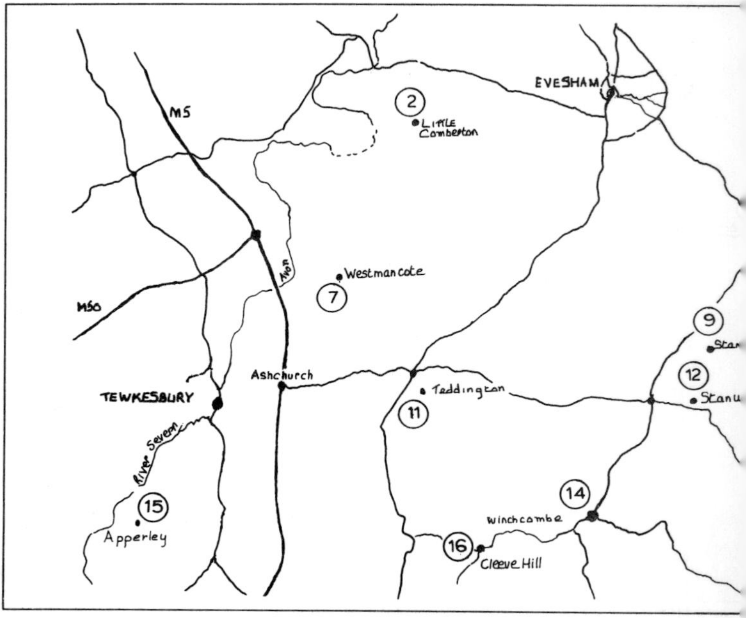

in newer industries in other parts of the country.

Consequently, the effects of the Industrial Revolution, which had brought about profound changes upon the landscape in other areas of the country, left the Cotswolds largely unscathed. It is thanks to this rapid decline in the prosperity of the area during the eighteenth and early nineteenth centuries that the Cotswolds remains today a region of rolling English countryside, interrupted at intervals by villages and towns characterised by a wealth of architecture which is pleasant and acceptable to the eye: ancient, undisturbed churches, rows of irregular cottages and the fine houses in acres of parkland built by the once wealthy merchants.

The name Cotswolds well describes the area as a whole. The word "wold" meant "upland common" in old English and the derivation of "Cot" is believed to have come from a word meaning an enclosure for sheep. Another theory as to the origin of the region's name is that a Saxon leader who farmed up around the

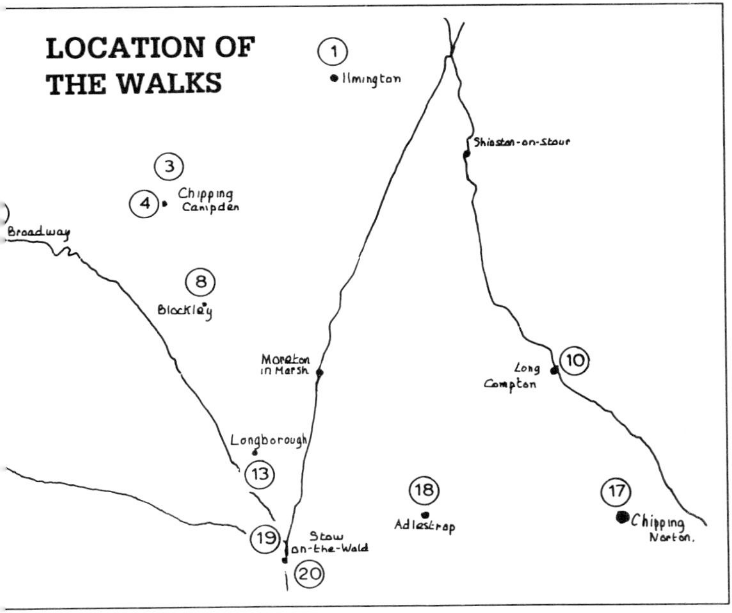

source of the river Windrush had the name "Cod" pronounced "Code" and the land was known as Code's High Land. Thus, in later centuries by combination of all three we have "Cotswolds" being applied to the whole area not just to the area around the headwaters of the Windrush.

Why Walk in the Cotswolds?

The Cotswold region is certainly one of the most popular of England's designated Areas of Outstanding Natural Beauty. It has been a source of inspiration for artists who have striven to capture the feeling and atmosphere of its landscape and architecture on canvas, just as writers and poets have tried to capture its unique qualities in the verbal imagery of their poetry and prose.

During the last half century, the family car and the tour bus have allowed many visitors access to this and other parts of our country that had previously been out of reach. Many people now speed through the countryside viewing the scenery through the windows of a car or coach. They may stop for morning coffee at Bibury, a stroll around the town of Burford, lunch at Stow-on-the Wold, cream tea at Chipping Camden, and, after a dash around Broadway, they head for home having "done" the Cotswolds. Few of these people, though enchanted by what they have seen, have had the opportunity to experience the full magnitude of the beauty of the landscape through which they have been whisked. All they have seen is a fleeting glimpse of some of the most popular Cotswold towns.

This is a pity indeed, for the Cotswold region offers a wealth of opportunities to escape from the pressure and pace of the twentieth-century urban living and to retreat back into an area in which the destructive aspects of development have not left their mark.

To experience the Cotswold region fully, to learn of its history, to be enticed by its charm and to revel in its peace and beauty, one must abandon the wheel and take to one's feet.

The Cotswolds must surely have everything that makes for good and interesting walking. Although it lacks in high moorland, mountains and the drama associated with such spectacular scenery, it does have the ideal combination of ingredients for the walker who likes to discover and explore at the same time. It is a fine mix of hills, valleys, woods, farmland, water meadows, ancient tracks, paths and lanes linking picturesque villages and towns of mellow honey coloured stone. The whole region, being steeped in history, is as rich and colourful as anywhere in England.

About These Walks

The walks in these books do not confine themselves to the boundaries of the designated Cotswolds Area of Outstanding Natural Beauty. This area is covered in detail but a number of additional peripheral regions of interest are also included.

Routes suggested start at tiny Ilmington close to Shipston on Stour in the north and stretch down to Wiltshire's Castle Combe in the south. To the west the walks will take you to Stinchcombe within sight of the River Severn, whilst the area around Woodstock in Oxfordshire is also visited in the east.

In planning these walks I have endeavoured to suit all tastes, with both walking and places of interest the major objectives. Some walks have been included just for the sheer beauty of the countryside through which they pass, whilst others have been included because they give good browsing opportunities down village streets, over ancient sites or in historical churches.

Each walk has straightforward instructions: an outline route, followed by a simple and easy to follow numbered set of instructions which tie in with a route map. All the walks detailed are circular and in most cases where I feel that clear instructions can be given for parking I have provided them. Details of Places and Points of Interest Along the Way are also given. The number of the appropriate Ordnance Survey Landranger map is given for each walk, together with the Grid Reference for the start.

The Walker's Rights on Access to the Cotswolds Paths

The right of way for the walker is along a *footpath, bridleway* or *byway*. Horseriders also have access to *bridleways*, as do pedal cyclists. The *byway* may be used by all those already mentioned with the addition of the motor vehicle. On all three you may walk your dog.

Footpaths crossing fields which have been ploughed must be made good by the farmer to a minimum width of one metre, within a maximum of two weeks. Similarly, farmers must prevent a crop from making the path difficult to follow. Footpaths along the edges of fields are the farmer's responsibility to clear to 1.5 metres wide. If the footpath is obstructed, eg. by barbed wire, you have the right to remove sufficient of the obstruction to allow access but the matter should be reported to the highway authority and to the Ramblers' Association. Cows and horses in fields are not considered to be an obstruction to the walker, but bulls of certain breeds - British Friesian, British Holstein, Ayrshire, Dairy Shorthorn, Kerry, Jersey and Guernsey - should not be in fields through which a public footpath runs. All other bulls, unless with heifers or cows, are also banned.

When reporting any obstruction on a public right of way give the grid reference, the date and all relevant information. You may find the following address useful: Ramblers' Association, 1-5 Wandsworth Road, London, SW8 2XX (Tel: 071 582 6878).

1: Ilmington

Map Landranger:	151
Start:	GR: SP 210 433
Distance:	$1^{1}/_{2}$ miles

Ilmington is a pretty village packed with interest. This short walk takes us up behind the village, through the fields to the ancient water source and uses well marked footpaths. It continues past the hurdle maker's workshop, the church and the mediaeval fish ponds and with two pubs in the villages what a could be a better way to spend a winter's day?

Route

1 At Ilmington, park beside the sloping green on the top of which can be seen the war memorial. At the bottom of the green is a water faucet whose inscription reads: "O All Ye Fountains Bless Ye The Lord". The tablet commemorates the exertions of those who provided the "blessing" of pure water for the inhabitants of Ilmington and is dated 1864.

2. With your back to the water faucet turn left, follow the road round passing Cuckoo Cottage (left). Pass the road junction (right) and walk up the hill a short distance turning right up the footpath, indicated by three arrow markers. Cross the stile at the top of the path and bear slightly left across the field to the stile in the hedge opposite.

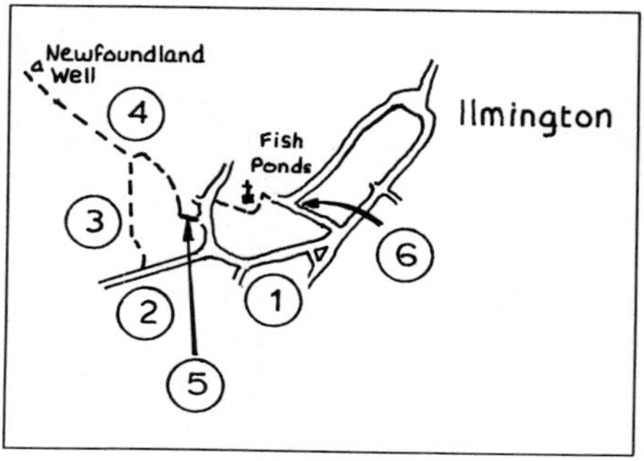

3. Cross the stile, turn right skirting

the field to the next white arrow marker, then continue across the field by way of the stiles following the white arrow markers until the Newfoundland Well is reached.

4. To return to the village retrace your steps until you reach the stile with two yellow arrow markers, follow the left one through a wooden gate and down the track passing between the houses. Lower down turn left to join the road.

5. To the right is the hurdle maker's workshop where we turn left. Shortly take the footpath (right) to the church. Pass the church, turn left, follow the path around (left) then (right) past the cottages and with the mediaeval fish lakes (left).

St Mary the Virgin, Ilmington

Ilmington village green, Cuckoo Cottage is to the right

6. Turn left, with the ditch (left), and stone buildings (right). When lower green is reached with the Howard Arms ahead, turn right, walk along the road soon passing the Red Lion (right) then taking the right fork signposted Campden to return to your parking place at Upper Green.

Places and Points of Interest Along the Way

ILMINGTON

Tucked away under the northern extremities of the Cotswold escarpment and lying a few miles from the Fosse Way is Ilmington,

One of the few thatched cottages left in Ilmington overlooks the mediaeval fish ponds

a picturesque village of part thatch/part timber framed cottages, generally acknowledged as being the home of Cotswold Morris dancing.

The parish church of St Mary the Virgin has a Norman tower claimed to be one of the finest in South Warwickshire. Over the church porch is the coat of arms of Simon de Montfort, at one time the church patron, whilst inside much evidence can be found of the church's Norman origins. This ancient church has been restored and modified throughout history, the most recent phase being during the 1930s when much replacement of the furnishings occurred. This was supervised by one of the most competent woodcarvers of the period, Robert Thomson of Kilburn in Yorkshire, and throughout the building he left no less than eleven examples of his "signature", the carved mouse, on pews, doors and even the pulpit.

Near to Bury Orchard are two ponds, the lower is thought to have originated during mediaeval times, whilst the higher L-shaped pond is perhaps part of the moat of the former Manor House of which there are, alas, no visible remains. Close by however is the present day manor and the Dower House.

During the nineteenth century, the village was well known to the horse racing fraternity, for here Manor House Farm stabled the Wilson's Grand National winners. After a number of years use as a winter home to the local dairy herd, the stables were converted in the 1970s to private dwellings.

Just behind the village school is Newfoundland Well where, in 1685, one Sam Derham wrote: "This spa water drank will help to cleanse and purifie the blood." Fortunately for today's villagers, the spring at not too distant Leamington developed along much more commercialised lines during later times when "taking the waters" for health reasons became very popular with the gentry, with the result that Ilmington was not too exposed to the Victorian development that engulfed Leamington Spa.

As time changes so many of our village communities, it is good to know that some places and some crafts still continue much as they did in the past; at Ilmington for instance, the village hurdlemaker still makes his hurdles in much the same way as they have been made for generations before.

2: The Combertons, Bredon Hill, Elmley Castle

Map Landranger:	150
Start:	GR: SO 955 422
Distance:	$6^{3}/_{4}$ miles

Climbing steeply out of Great Comberton, this route continues along the ridge of the Bredon Hill from where there are extensive views over the Vale of Evesham and the River Avon. The attractive village of Elmley Castle, sheltering in the lee of the hill, has two pubs - the Elizabeth of England, near the church and another, more modern hostelry, overlooking the village green.

Route

1. In Great Comberton park in Church Street. Walk up the hill by the church (right) and at the road junction go left following the public footpath signposted to Overbury. Cross the field and at the metal barns turn right, passing between the farm buildings to join the track ahead.
2. Continue along the track until it ends and the incline increases. Eventually cross into the bottom of a V-shaped field with wire fences left and right. Walk ahead with the remains of a stone wall (right), passing a spring (right) and a wire fence (left). Continue with the wire fence close (left) as the climb becomes steeper towards the top of the hill. At the top the Banbury Stone is about $^{1}/_{4}$ mile (right) should you wish to see it.
3. To continue with the walk turn left and walk along the ridge of Bredon Hill with the stone wall (right) until the wall ends, when you continue along a track with a wire fence (right). When the crossing of four tracks is reached, with wooden fences (left), go down (left) passing through the gate displaying blue, yellow and Wychavon Way arrow markers and follow the path down through the woods.

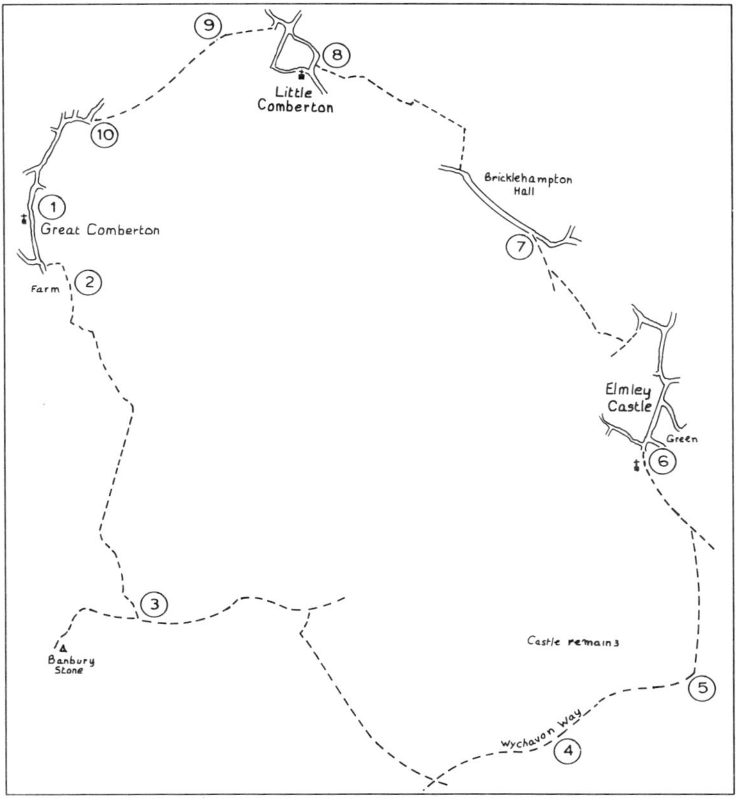

4. Continue down the track indicated by the markers, passing the remains of Elmley Castle (left). Go through the wooden gate ahead (left) beside the horse jump. Continue down the hill aiming towards the bottom right of the field, crossing the stile and footbridge then turn left.

5. Walk along the left side of the field, with the ditch and wire fence (left), following the path round until a stile (left) is reached. Cross it, walk over the small field to exit over a further stile onto a pathway. Walk, by a small lake (left), into the

Cottages near the green at Elmley Castle

churchyard and exit into the main street of Elmley Castle.

6. Walk down the main street, passing the Elizabeth of England (left), the village school (right) following the road round in the direction of the Combertons. After passing the last of the brick houses (left), turn left up the public right of way and go into the field. Walk straight ahead until you reach the stile (left). Turn 90° right here. Walk ahead, with the hedge close (left) and the road over to the right, until you cross a stile on to the road.

7. Turn left, pass Bricklehampton Hall (right) and where the road curves left, take the footpath indicated into the field (right). Cross the field, go over the stile and turn left walking with the hedge close (left), down the next field. At the bottom of the field turn sharp right, cross the stile with the footbridge (right) and walk parallel to the hedge (right) until the bottom of the field is reached. Go left until a metal fence is reached (right), pass through it, cross the small field then over a stile onto the road at Little Comberton.

8. Turn left, pass the Manor House (right), walk down Manor Lane (right), passing the Church of St Peter. At the road junction turn left along the road until the footpath signposted

Bricklehampton Hall, the Victorian mansion built in the Italian style

to Great Comberton (left) is reached. Cross the stile aiming diagonally right over the field to cross the footbridge in the right corner beside the telegraph pole.

9. Walk in line with the telegraph poles over the next two fields, leaving from the second field over the footbridge right of the last telegraph pole. Turn left off the footbridge and aim for the bottom right corner where you should exit onto the road at the footpath sign.

The Elizabeth of England Inn, Elmley Castle

Timber frame cottages in Manor Lane, Little Comberton

10. Turn left and follow the road past the war memorial (right) returning to your starting point in Church Street.

Places and Points of Interest Along the Way

BREDON HILL

Ancient earth works dating from both Roman times and earlier periods in history adorn the 980ft high mushroom like summit of Bredon Hill as it rises from the flatland of the Vale of Evesham. It has been described by some as looking like a stranded whale dotted with copse and woodland and criss-crossed with tracks.

In days gone by, due to its rather isolated position and its ability to attract cloud, it was always a good weather indicator, in fact it

Manor Lane, Little Comberton

was used as a local barometer and an old rhyme goes as follows:

When Bredon Hill puts on its hat,
ye men of the vale beware of that.
When Bredon Hill doth clear appear,
ye men of the vale have nought to fear.

The eighteenth-century Parson's Folly was at one time reputed to be the home of a raw rabbit eating hermit, but in earlier times the land surrounding the folly formed the ramparts of an Iron Age hill fort. The remains of fifty men were found when the hill fort was excavated, it was assumed that these were the defenders who had been left where they fell at their last battle. Also here is the 14ft high by 60ft round Banbury Stone which it is considered may possibly have been a Roman altar or a Druids sacrificial stone.

THE COMBERTONS

The Comberton villages, one "Great" and one "Little" are situated on the very edge of the Cotswold heartland. Here, unlike the villages to the south, can be found half timbered buildings made with roofs of thatch together with the local stone for which the Cotswolds is well renowned. Quite common in days gone by, but today alas something of a rarity, were dovecotes. At Great Comberton where the picturesque village church dates from the thirteenth century, there are two dovecotes. Little Comberton, the sister village, is similar in its architecture and strangely enough also has two dovecotes. Parts of the church here date back to Norman times as do so many other village churches in the Cotswolds. St Peters, however, is believed to stand on the site of a Roman temple, as a number of artifacts associated with that period have been found in the churchyard. Inside the church, the words of one of the First World War's most famous poets, Rupert Brooks, read:

If I should die, think only this of me;
That there's some corner of a foreign field
that is forever England.

A fine epitaph to three local men who died in foreign parts.

ELMLEY CASTLE

Elmley Castle is another black and white picture of timber framed houses. Here a small stream flows down the main street and the entrance to many of the cottages is consequently across a small footbridge. The Norman castle, after which the village was named, was destroyed by Henry VII and little remains today. The visit made by Elizabeth I to the village on 20 August 1577 is remembered in the name of the village inn, the Elizabeth of England.

In the village church the base of the font is thirteenth century while the octagonal bowl and the most unusual sundials date from the sixteenth century.

The old sundial in front of the church at Elmley Castle

3: *Mickleton, The Hidcotes, Chipping Campden*

Map Landranger:	151
Start:	GR: SP 162 436
Distance:	9 miles

This walk over undulating countryside, links tiny picture postcard hamlets with the formality of Chipping Campden. It is suggested that ample time should be allowed to explore the many interesting aspects of Chipping Campden which, together with a choice of several good pubs, tea shops and restaurants, combine to make an ideal half-way stopping place.

Route

1. At MICKLETON find Lloyds Bank in the main street, the B4081, just across from which is a telephone box at the junction of a side road leading to the church. Close to the telephone box is the road sign to Broad Marston; park in this side road. Walk up this road passing the church (left) and Field House (right) before going through the kissing gate into the field.
2. Walk towards the hedge ahead, then turn right and go through the kissing gate (left) - Heart of England Way - following the trees and hedge close (right) then past the stile (right), before going through the gateway (ahead) with the blue marker. Beyond the wire fence is a stream. Follow this fence until a gateway is reached (right) with a blue arrow marker, then cross the field and enter Kiftsgate Court Park.
3. Climb to the top of the field, pass through the gateway marked with two arrows, one yellow, one blue. Continue up the hill, turning steep right at the stone wall (ahead) and leaving the field through a wooden gateway at the Kiftsgate Park Lodge and onto the road at a bridleway sign.
4. Cross the road and walk in the direction of Hidcote Gardens.

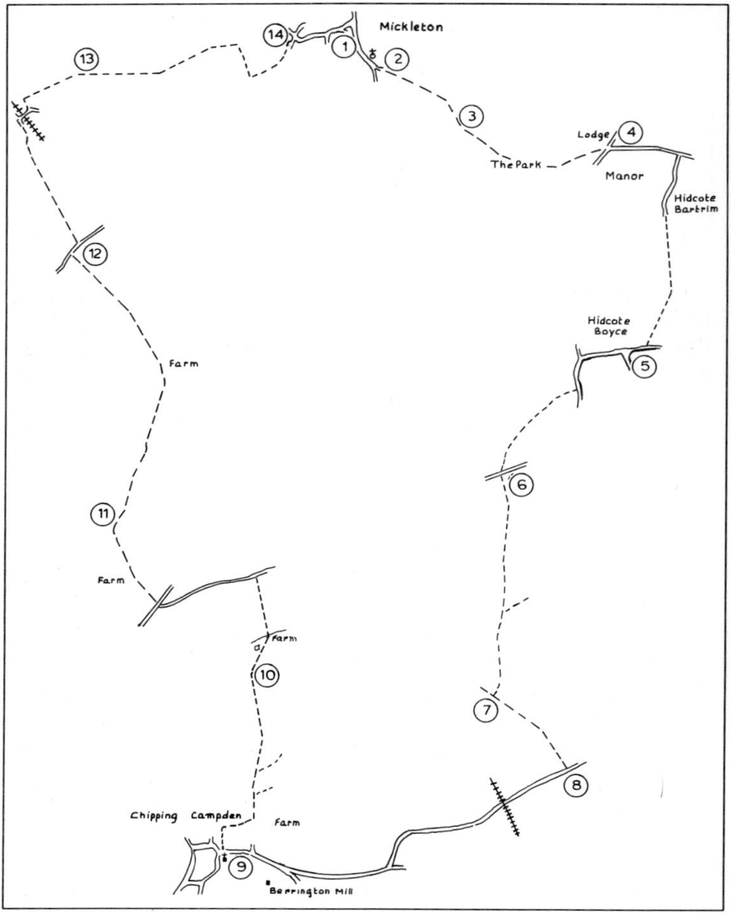

Just before the car park, turn right between the avenue of trees passing Hidcote House (right) and the tiny hamlet of Hidcote Bartrim. At the end of the lane and with a barn (right), take the footpath straight ahead across the fields. Cross a ditch then bear slightly right towards the farm buildings (ahead).

Cottages and farm buildings at Hidcote Boyce

5. Exit through the gate between the farm buildings and into a lane, turning right to walk through Hidcote Boyce. Turn left at the T-junction. Shortly after passing a pair of semi-detached houses (left), go over the stile (right) with an arrow marker. Cross the field ahead, over a stile with a yellow marker, across the next field before following the line of a hedge (left), leaving the field via a gate and onto the road.
6. Cross the road, walk down the field to the right of the metal barn ahead, aiming for the gate (with an arrow marker) at the end of the next field. Go over the footbridge with arrow marker, into another field, keeping the ditch on the right, until you can cross into the field (right) by way of a footbridge.
7. Turn left, as indicated by the yellow arrow markers, with the ditch and hedge now on your left. Cross a footbridge, walk along the bottom of another field before taking the footbridge with blue arrow markers (left) into the final field. Walk straight ahead, aiming left of the telegraph pole. Leave the field using the footbridge spanning the ditch, walk up the track with the

hedge (left) towards the houses (ahead) and exit onto the road.

8. Turn right, walk down the road, go over the level crossing gradually climbing towards Chipping Campden and at the junction of Station Road and the B4035, turn right towards the church tower passing the lovely old Berrington Mill across the fields (left).
9. If you wish to explore Chipping Campden, pass the church, bear left passing the almshouses (right), then turn right into the town. To continue the walk, turn right at the church, walk up the driveway towards Chipping Campden School and go through the gateway in the metal fence (right). Turn left and walk between the fence (left) and hedge (right). Follow the path around to the right with the school (left), turning left until you have passed beyond the school grounds.
10. Go over the stile towards the farm buildings (ahead), passing between the farm house and the buildings then join the track (ahead). Cross the ditch and walk down the field with the hedge close by on the right. At the road turn left. At the road junction walk straight ahead where the notice reads Private Road and after passing the farm buildings (left), the bridleway goes right, off the tarmac surface.
11. Follow the bridleway round to the right leading to a wooden gate with a blue bridleway sign. Continue ahead, going down the hill, still following the blue markers. With Middle Norton Farm (right), cross the track and aim for the right end of the copse ahead. Veer slightly right across the next field with the copse (left), cross the next field with the hedge close (right).
12. At the road, turn right then take the bridleway (left) over the fields with the hedge (right). Continue until the lane is reached, then turn right going across the railway bridge taking the footpath (left), aiming left of the metal barn. Walk down the path with a new tree plantation (left) and a wire fence (right), following the arrow markers and aiming for the church steeple ahead.
13. Walk down the field to cross the stile and footbridge at the bottom. Go over the next stile and walk ahead, keeping a ditch (left) and Mickleton comes into view ahead (right). At the end

Berrington Mill

of the field, turn slightly right to cross the stile ahead, then go right over another stile. Pass in front of a row of brick farm buildings, go over a footbridge spanning a ditch. Follow the path left around the field, eventually exiting into a path behind the bungalows.

14. Bear right through the housing estate, passing the Butcher's Arms (left) then go left past the Three Ways Hotel and at the T-junction, turn right. A short distance along the main street will bring you back to the starting point.

The fountain, Mickleton

Places and Points of Interest Along the Way

CHIPPING CAMPDEN

For me Chipping Campden rates well amongst the most popular towns of the Cotswolds, reflecting its immense past wealth generated from wool. Its very name is connected with trading - "Chipping" meaning market. Lying in a hollow below the high Dovers Hill, it became one of the main markets and collecting places for wool during the fourteenth century but even as far back as Doomsday, it had around 300 inhabitants. Its solid and splendid looking houses, together with the great perpendicular church, give it a quite unique appearance when compared with other Cotswold towns.

"The flower of the wool merchants of all England" is how William Grevel, the town's greatest benefactor who died in 1401, is described. His memorial brass is in St James Church where much rebuilding was carried out during the fifteenth century and where the tower is considered to be as fine as any in the Cotswolds. The nave, dating from around 1488 was probably built by the same master mason who produced the nave at Northleach, another wealthy wool town during its heyday. There are recumbent effigies

The Market Hall, Chipping Campden

from 1629 of the first Viscount Campden and his wife in state robes amongst other local dignitaries represented in the church. Sir Thomas, Lord of the Manor of Campden and First Governor of the East India Company also lies there. In the south-west corner of the church, a set of steps lead to a small fourteenth-century tower where the Muniment Room - formerly a schoolroom, - houses all the church's treasures and documents.

The town's great mansion, Old Campden House, with its gateway close to the church, was built in 1613 for the Viscount of Campden. Unfortunately it was burnt to the ground during the Civil War and very little is left today. On the curving High Street are numerous buildings erected at various times, one of the oldest being Grevel House just opposite Church Street, which dates from the fourteenth century. While the Woolstapler's Hall just opposite is from the same period, Bedfont House is claimed to be the finest eighteenth-century house in the street, close by is Sherborn House with the Campden Car Collection of historic cars. The Market Hall, built in 1627 to house the butter, cheese and poultry market (and now owned by the National Trust), stands on its own in the middle of the street.

During the eighteenth and nineteenth centuries when other towns were developing their milling potential with the aid of water power, Chipping Campden declined in importance as no suitable water source was at hand. However, during the early 1900s C.R.Ashbee, a disciple of William Morris and a follower of Ruskin, came to the town with his Guild of Handicrafts. Since then, arts and crafts have thrived here and the Campden Trust, formed in 1929, has done much to preserve and restore the local architecture.

Another less cultural association with the town is the peculiar Cotswold sport of shin-kicking. Contests are held around the last Friday in May and are a left over from the Dover Games, named after Captain Dover who inaugurated the Cotswold

Games back in 1612. In those days the games included horse racing, cock fighting, wrestling and bull-baiting. By comparison, today's events are quite modest.

MICKLETON AND THE HIDCOTES

Lying below the Cotswold Edge, Mickleton is one of the northern Cotswold villages that combine so well a mix of thatch, timber frame and stone buildings. Its medieval church of St Lawrence has a large porch consisting of two stories which dates from the seventeenth century, while the church font was first used in 1661.

Chipping Campden

Almost at the conclusion of the walk and opposite the Three Ways Hotel, we pass the village fountain. The inscription points out that water was brought to the village in 1875 and that the fountain built in the memory of Sir James Steel Graves-Bart was designed by William Burgess.

Not far from Mickleton is the Manor of Hidcote with its famous gardens, now owned by the National Trust. The house dates from the seventeenth century and was bought in 1907 by the American, Lawrence Johnston who developed this horticultural masterpiece. Close by are more gardens at Kiftsgate House and about half a mile distant is the fine sixteenth-century Hidcote House.

The tiny hamlets of Hidcote Bartrim and Hidcote Boyce are both a scattering of picturesque cottages that would do justice to any chocolate box lid.

Hidcote Bartrim

4: Chipping Campden, Dovers Hill

Map Landranger:	151
Start:	GR: SP 152 392
Distance:	4³/₄ miles

This walk is only a short one which could easily be made during dry winter weather; It is hilly but stimulating. From history steeped Chipping Campden, our route takes us steadily up to and along the top of Dovers Hill from where the views to the north and north-west are breathtaking. The second half of the walk entails a steep climb up the bridleway, along the western edge of Weston Park; this part can be very muddy in wet weather.

Route

1. At Chipping Campden, park in the square near the Cotswold Hotel. Walk down the main street in the direction of Weston Sub-Edge, passing Sheep Street (left). At the Volunteer Inn (left), turn right at St Catherine's RC Church, walk up the street

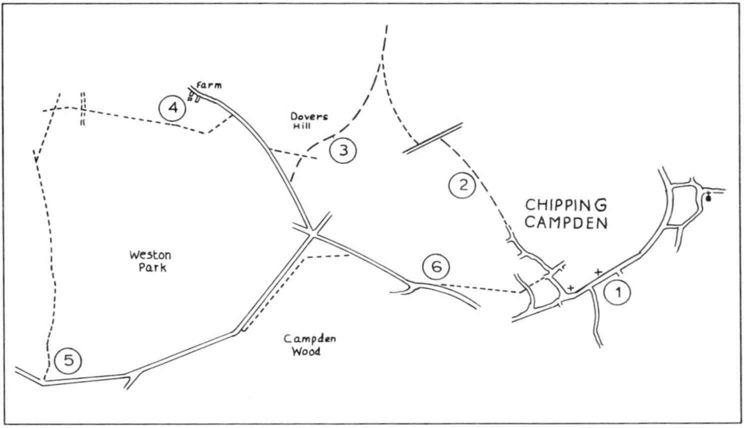

Up to Dovers Hill past Littleworth Cottage

past Littleworth Cottage (left) following the Cotswold Way sign up the hill.

2. On reaching the farm buildings (left), cross the stile with the yellow arrow marker. Continue up the footpath and at the road turn left, then first right, signposted Cotswold Way - Dovers Hill. When Dovers Hill is reached, turn left and with the hedge (left) walk along the ridge, passing the Dovers Hill National Trust sign on the stone pillar (right).

3. About halfway to the road, turn right, walk towards the left edge of the trees (ahead) to join the track leading to a gateway onto the road. Turn right, walk down the hill and take the next footpath (left), over the stile. Walk across the fields gradually bearing right to cross the stile in the fence (ahead), with the farm building (right), close to the road.

4. Continue down, cross the stile, then along the track (ahead) to follow the footpath signs to the bottom left of the field. Here there are two stiles (with arrow markers); cross the first and walk up the field with the ditch running down (right). Cross the next stile and footbridge (marked with a blue arrow),

turning left onto the bridleway to climb up through the woods to the road.

5. Turn left onto the road, walking in the direction of Chipping Campden. At the road junction continue left and where the road bears left, follow the Cotswold Way sign down to the right. Keep going straight ahead parallel to the road (left) and just before the crossroads sign there is a wooden gateway. At this point turn down (right) and bearing at about 45°, walk in line with Chipping Campden Church (which can be seen through the trees ahead) to exit eventually into Dyer's Lane.
6. Turn right passing Woodhouse Cottage (right) at the lane junction and take the footpath (left) signposted to Chipping Campden. Then turn right into the field, bearing slightly left away from the lane and exit between the houses into the roadway. Cross into the footpath between the houses opposite and at the next junction, turn right towards the Volunteer Inn from where you can retrace your steps back to the starting place.

Places and Points of Interest Along the Way

DOVERS HILL

Bought by the National Trust in 1928, Dovers Hill is a favourite area when winter is over with local kite flying enthusiasts. Due to its high, unsheltered position, it is also a fine vantage point and affords an excellent panorama across the Vale of Evesham below.

Its name is derived from Robert Dover who was a successful lawyer during the 1600s and was the founder of the Cotswold Games which are held in the surrounding area. In those early days the games were much more rough and tumble than present day sporting events and consisted of such contests as wrestling, horse racing, stick fighting, bear baiting, cock fighting and perhaps the most unusual sport of shin-kicking. The games, even mentioned by Shakespeare, were so well known in their day that it is said that King James gave his approval by presenting Robert Dover with a suit and feathered hat to wear when pronouncing the games "open". In 1852 however, when the supporters were frequently becoming drunk and out of hand, the games were disbanded. As recently as 1951 the games were revived in a much modified form for the Festival of

Britain and are now held around the last Friday in May. They are followed the day after by the Scuttlebrook Wake, the festival at Chipping Campden.

Seventeenth century almshouses, Chipping Campden

5: Broadway, Saintbury, Willersey

Map Landranger:	150
Start:	GR: SP 100 376
Distance:	6 miles

The hills above Saintbury afford extensive views across the Vale of Evesham to the Malvern Hills and even the mountains of Wales, but as they can be very bleak after catching the snow in winter, the walk is best undertaken in good weather.

Route

1. Park in the public car park at Leamington Road in Broadway. Go out of the car park, turn left into Leamington Road and walk to the T-junction with the main road. Turn left and walk up the hill, until Bibsworth Lane (left) is reached with the sign reading: Public Bridleway Willersey and Saintbury Church. Go down the lane to the end and before the metal barns ahead are reached go through the white gate (right) into the field. Walk diagonally left aiming for the gap in the hedge to the right of the large tree (ahead).
2. Go through the next gate turning diagonally left of the telegraph pole and walk ahead to commence the ascent following the blue arrow markers. Crossing a private road, continue to the golf club notice at the fence.
3. Pass through the gate, turn left then bear right and follow the path close to the fence (left) with the golf course (right), until the road is reached. Cross the road and go over the stile following the yellow arrow markers down the hill.
4. Go left of the wire fence ahead and continue down the hill with Willersey down to the left. Cross the stile (right), descend through the woods, exit over a further stile and follow the right of way via the gate into the churchyard.

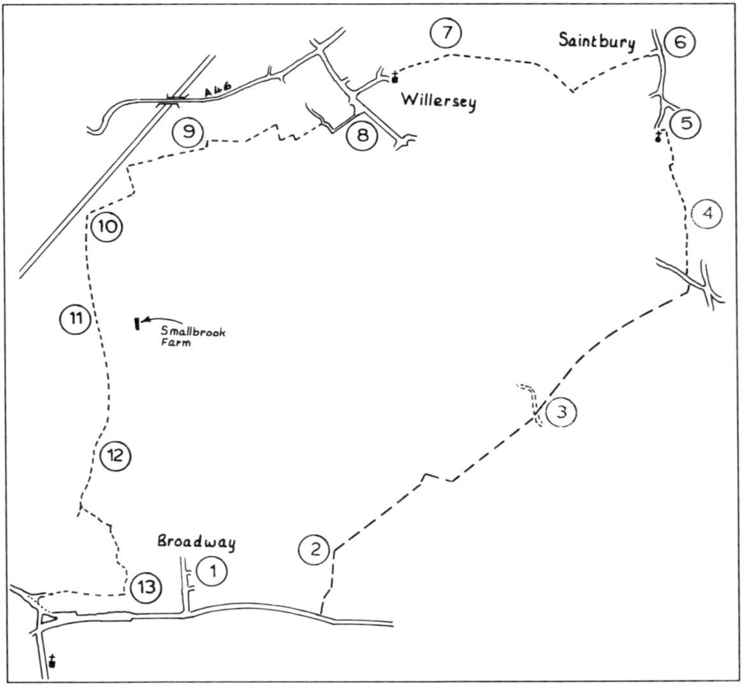

5. Leave the churchyard by way of the front gate and walk down the driveway to the road. Follow the road down the hill until a footpath sign is reached (right). Turn left, pass the telephone box and walk between the houses to the stile (left) of Field Cottage (right).

6. Cross the stile, go diagonally left down the field, cross a second stile, then pass a wire fence (left). At the stile ahead yellow markers indicate left and right, go right following the arrow markers through the fields until the next stile with two arrows is crossed, turn left.

7. Walk a short distance with the hedge (left), pass through the gate ahead and continue following the arrows. Pass through

Saxon Sundial at St Nicholas' Church, Saintbury

the churchyard into Church Street with the post office and school to the right. At the main road with the Bell Inn (left), turn left then cross the road and walk up to the next trackway (right). This goes to the village hall, in front of which the public right of way is indicated by the sign.

8. Continue along the right of way, walking through the housing estate, until the path joins a road at right angles. Ahead of you to the right is a tarmac drive beside a bungalow, go down it and through a metal gate. Turn diagonally right, cross the stile and walk close to the wire fence (right) and cross a second stile.

9. After passing the metal barns (right) you can see to the right the bridge carrying the A46 road over the disused railway line. The path continues with the disused railway (right) until you reach the corner of the field. Here is a stile (right) where you turn left.

10. Go over the footbridge (right), turn left and continue with the brook running left, cross a further footbridge and continue ahead with the brook (left). As you approach Smallbrook Farm over to the left you will reach a ditch at right angles to your path, turn right and walk until you pass the second hedge going off left.

11. At the end of the hedge the right of way continues straight ahead across the field to the tall tree. Cross the stile that has yellow arrow markers on it and onto the track. Walk ahead with a wooden fence (left) until a track at right angles is

St Nicholas' Church, Saintbury

reached. Turn right and at the hedge (left) walk towards the houses.

12. Just before the first house turn right over a footbridge and continue behind the houses. Turn left before you reach the stile ahead and continue behind the housing estate following the path round until after passing through a wooden gate into an orchard exit between small stable buildings onto a track.

13. At Bell Court Yard turn right and continue down the track eventually exiting onto the main street with the Coach House (left) across the road. Turn left and walk up Broadway's main street to return to Leamington Road car park.

Cottages at Broadway

Places and Points of Interest Along the Way

SAINTBURY

Mentioned in the Doomsday Book in 1086 as Swainsbury, Saintbury sits on the very edge of the Cotswold escarpment where it begins to curve eastward. For those interested after the descent from the higher ground the church is well worth a visit. Dedicated to St Nicholas, the patron saint of Russia, choirboys, children and sailors, it was founded by the monks of Pershore. The church is unusual in that it has both a spire and a tower. The graceful spire dates from the fourteenth century, and below it, on the south transept, is the tower - unusual as the usual position is at the west end of the church. Outside, on the south wall of the nave a Norman doorway, with a lozenge patterned tympanum above it, has been blocked up. Above this the sundial is Saxon and is thought to be pre-1050. It has three radii with a cross at each end, thereby indicating the times of services of Mass, Sext and Compline.

The north doorway is Norman and the door itself is of oak, carved by the Campden Guild with an effigy of the patron saint. The ironwork and joinery is typical of the high standard of craftsmanship of the arts and crafts movement. Inside, the fine barrel-vaulted ceiling of the chancel is ascribed also to the Campden Guild. The graceful looking font is quite unusual, a combination of Norman, Early English and Tudor styles; it is assumed that it dates from about 1500 to 1560.

WILLERSEY

Willersey is situated at the foot of the Cotswold scarp and it is here that the Abbots of Evesham had their summer residence at the Manor House. Today, Willersey has wide greens on each side of the busy main road. A duck pond is situated close to the seventeenth-century Pool House while just across the road stands the Bell Inn.

Abbot Batton, who died in 1418 was the designer of the massive pillars that support the tower of the medieval church of St Peter, the tower being placed rather unusually at the centre of the church. It is a solid, robust building and a typically good example of church architecture of the period from the twelfth to sixteenth century, whilst still retaining traces of the Saxon and Norman styles.

6: Broadway, Broadway Tower, Fish Hill

Map Landranger:	150
Start:	GR: SP 096 375
Distance:	$4^{1}/_{4}$ miles

This route is just about as steep as you can find anywhere in the Cotswolds. It takes the walker, by way of a footpath, from the centre of Broadway to the top of Fish Hill, returning through woods and down the fields to the top of the main street. It is a walk that is worth making just for the views alone, but the uphill path can be heavy going in wet conditions.

Route

1. At Broadway park in the car park at the rear of the church. Access is by way of Church Close. At the opposite end of the

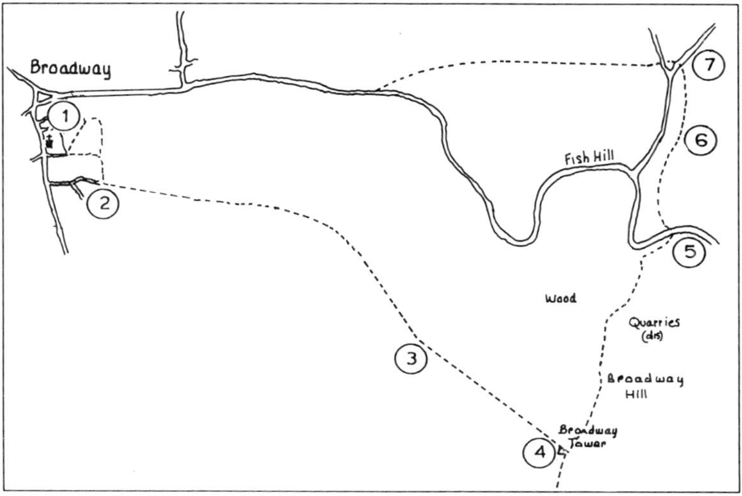

car park to the shopping centre is an exit over a stile onto a pathway, take it and turn left. Pass through the trees with a metal fence (right).

2. Pass through a wooden gate turning right and with a metal barn (left) cross a stile then a footbridge over a stream. Turn left and walk straight ahead up the fields crossing the stiles and following the arrow markers, keeping the stream on the right.

3. At the National Trust sign Clump Farm (right), cross the stile and bear right up the track with the dry stone wall (left) and shortly the Broadway Tower comes into view amidst the trees ahead.

4. On reaching the Tower go down (left) through a wooden gate and walk along a high ridge. Cross the stiles and at the fork of the tracks in the beech woods go right, then pass through a disused quarry.

5. At the road with the Fish Inn (right) cross to the Cotswold Way

The footpath down to Broadway

sign and take the left path down through the trees. On reaching three steps (right) walk up them and continue up and around (right) through the trees following the arrow markers.

6. At a signpost (right) indicating the footpath to Broadway go left and walk along the edge of the woods, with farmland over the stone wall (right). On reaching the metal buildings (right) the path zig-zags down (left) to the road.
7. Cross the road at the junction, then cross the stile signposted Broadway directly ahead, with Dormy House Hotel to the right and Fancombe House to the left. Walk down the fields following the arrow markers, cross over a stile onto the main road and walk in Broadway.

Places and Points of Interest Along the Way

BROADWAY, BROADWAY TOWER and FISH HILL

Broadway is perhaps the most perfect showpiece in all the Cotswolds, where many of the buildings in the wide main street date back 400 years or more. Claimed by some to be the most beautiful village in England, this is where the well kept gardens in front of the mellow stone houses, each with dormer in the roof and bow window below, reach out to the roadway and vie with each other to catch the visitors eye. Despite the tea shops, the inns and the antique shops, this large village has not been spoilt in order to pander to the day tripper, but most of the original features blend in well with the more recent additions.

Two of the oldest houses in the county of Worcestershire are here: the Priors Manse on the main street and the Abbots Grange below the green, both dating from the fourteenth century. Most of the houses however, were built during the seventeenth and eighteenth centuries when Broadway was a busy staging post on the route from London to Worcester, having at one time no less than twenty inns. Both Charles I and Cromwell are said to have stayed at the former White Hart Inn which dates from 1620 and is today known as The Lygon Arms. General Lygon, after whom the inn was renamed, was a local eccentric who had his estate planted with trees in the same formation as the troops at the Battle of Waterloo so he was able to re-enact the battle.

With the development of the railways in more recent times, the village's prosperity declined, only to be revived by the influence of William Morris. It is said that on one of his journeys from his residence at Kelmscott Manor to stay at the Broadway Tower during 1876, he passed through Burford and was appalled at the renovation work that was being carried out on the church. His words of disapproval were wasted on the vicar but soon after his arrival at Broadway, Morris did much to lay the foundations of the Society for the Protection of Ancient Monuments. He is reported to have said: "Old buildings are not in any sense our property to do with as we like. We are only the trustees for those who come after us".

Perhaps the best known of the local residents was Sir Thomas Philips, who died in 1872. He was a fanatical collector of books, his rather ambitious aim being to have a copy of every book in the world! At one time he lived at the nearby Broadway Tower, the second highest point in the Cotswolds, which it is thought was built in 1797 by the Earl of Coventry and from where, on a clear day, much of central England can be seen. The tower stands at the top of the 1,000ft high Fish Hill and is itself 65ft high.

Broadway Tower

7: Westmancote, Kemerton, Overbury

Map Landranger:	150
Start:	GR: SO 938 376
Distance:	5 miles

This level walk, passing through woodland and over farmland, links together the quiet and attractive villages of Westmancote, Kemerton and Overbury. This is, however, one of the few walks in this book without a pub along the route. Therefore, before turning left towards Overbury, it may be worth a small diversion to Conderton to obtain refreshments at the Yew Tree. For those who wish to visit the village of Bredon a footpath goes diagonally across the field from the south side of the Baptist Church at Westmancote. The alternative is to motor the short distance to Bredon on completion of the walk.

Route

1. Park your car near the Baptist Church at Westmancote. Walk south down the road away from the village. At the main road turn right in the direction of Tewkesbury, then go down the

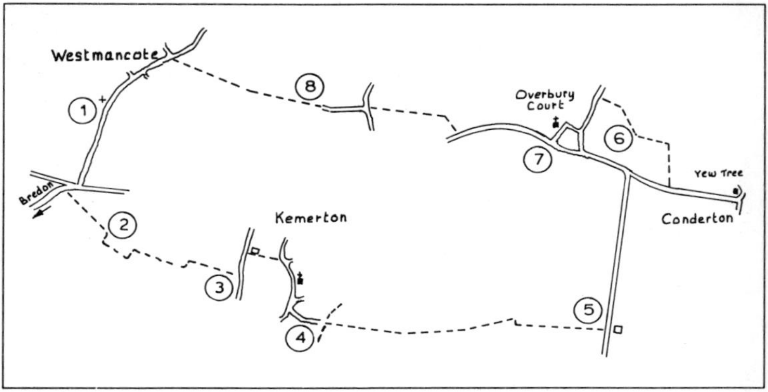

Overbury Court

footpath ahead (left) signposted to Kinsham.

2. Follow the path round right then left over the stile, left again walking along the left side of the field next to the wire fence with young trees beyond. Cross the track, continue ahead diagonally left. Half way down the field is a stile, cross it and follow the path (right) to the road.
3. At the road turn left and walk to the brick farm buildings (right). Turn right into the field passing left of the buildings and walking with a wire fence (right) until the road is reached by crossing the stile. Turn right, pass St Nicholas's Church (left) and take the second turning left. After passing the garden with a high wooden fence continue down the track bearing right at the end of a stone wall (left) then exit into a field.
4. Pass through a wooden gate where the right of way becomes a footpath and with a hedge (left) continue ahead for about $^{1}/_{2}$ mile. At the end of the field go over a stile (left) then right, pass through two wooden gates and turn left. Walking close to the hedge aim for the farm buildings across the road ahead.
5. Turn left, walk along the road to the T-junction. Turn right and

continue until the footpath sign (left) is reached. Cross the stile and walk ahead through the woods until the end of the wooden fence (left) is reached. Turn left, leave the woods and walk along with the wire fence (left) towards the buildings ahead.

6. At the bowling green (left) follow the path round (right) with the stone wall (left). Cross the stone stile onto the track which leads to the road at Overbury. Turn left, walk down the road turning into the next road (right). Pass the church (right) as you bear round left towards the main road.

7. Turn right and continue along the main road until it curves left. Go through the wooden gate (right) set into the stone wall. At the opposite left corner of the field go through the gate with the yellow arrow marker and walk straight ahead over the fields with a hedge (right). When the road is reached cross it and walk ahead down the lane past Kings Lea (left).

At Overbury

Overbury. The village stores and Post Office

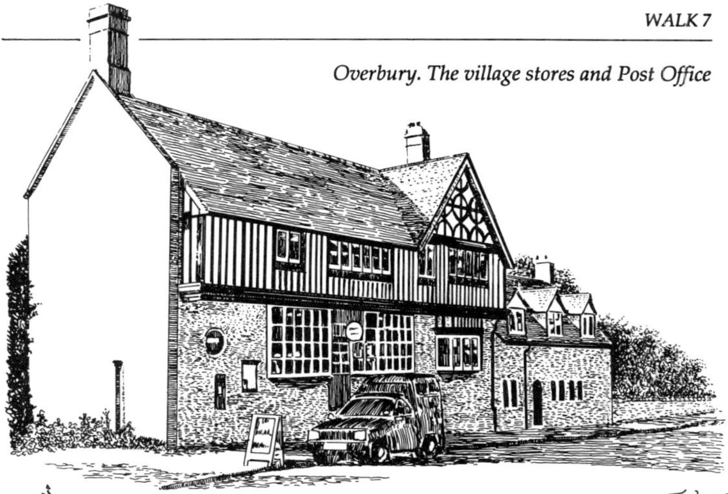

8. At Laurel Cottage continue ahead onto the public footpath indicating Westmancote 1/2 mile. Pass through a metal kissing gate, turn right then left across the fields with a hedge (right) to Westmancote. At the road turn left to the Baptist Church.

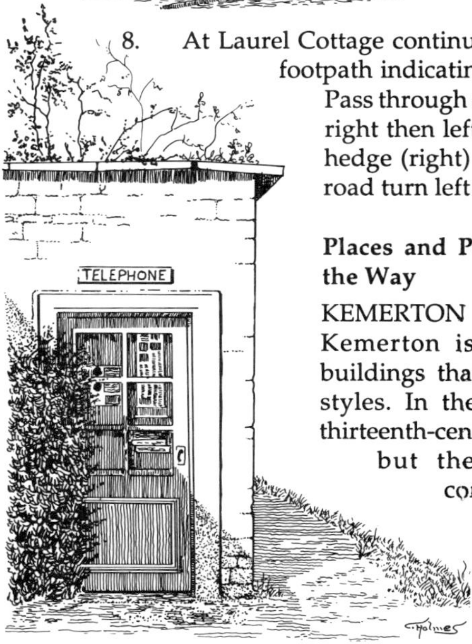

At Overbury the public telephone box is built into a garden wall

Places and Points of Interest Along the Way

KEMERTON

Kemerton is a large village with buildings that form fine contrasts of styles. In the church some original thirteenth-century work is still apparent but the church was almost completely rebuilt during the nineteenth century. Lower Mill Farm with its old water mill still surviving was once the home of the late John

Timber framed cottage at Kemerton

Moore, the country author probably best known for his novel *Elmbury*. The gardens of the priory are open to the public on certain days during the summer months.

OVERBURY

During 1723, John Martin of Martins, the banking family, came to live at Overbury Manor. Unfortunately it was burned down some fifteen years later following which, the present Overbury Court was built. At that time of course, the village looked quite different from today: far more industrialised with mills producing paper, flour and textiles. During the nineteenth century however, the industries closed down and Norman Shaw, one of the prominent architects of the period, was appointed to tidy the village up. Evidence of his effectiveness can be seen in the view of Overbury Court with its fine Georgian façade facing south towards the vale and its entrance gates bordered by the cottages to left and right.

Claimed, just as are other villages hereabouts, to be the prettiest in the country, Overbury is certainly one of the most delightful of

Cottages beside the main road at Overbury

those in the northern Cotswolds with its fine combination of stone and half timbered buildings. The lovely church of St Faiths, with its twelfth-century nave and tower of 300 years later, is idyllically placed in the village with a flight of steps leading up to a picturesque lych gate.

BREDON VILLAGE

There is much on offer at Bredon village if you choose to make the short journey here after completing the walk. It is a pleasing collection of many styles of architecture and is best explored on foot. Many different sizes and shapes of timber framed houses are to be found in Church Street. Close to the Fox and Hounds, while not too far from the right fork at the main road, are the Reed Almshouses. The main attraction of Bredon is the Tithe Barn, now owned by the National Trust. It dates from 1350 and was more likely to have been

used as a massive 130ft by 40ft store house for crops from Bredon Manor. The extra feature on this handsome piece of architecture is the Reeve's Office, atop the stone staircase from where there is an excellent view of the whole barn.

From the church, a lane runs down towards the Avon, affording good views over the flatland and along the river banks, a reminder that we are now very close to the north-westerly edge of the Cotswolds.

8: Blockley, Norcombe Wood, The Warren

Map Landranger:	151
Start:	GR: SP 165 349
Distance:	3 miles approx.

The large village of Blockley sits in the valley of Blockley brook. This walk follows a gently undulating route through the wooded countryside, the colours of which are most spectacular in the spring or autumn.

Route

1. At Blockley, park in Bell Lane near the British Legion building.

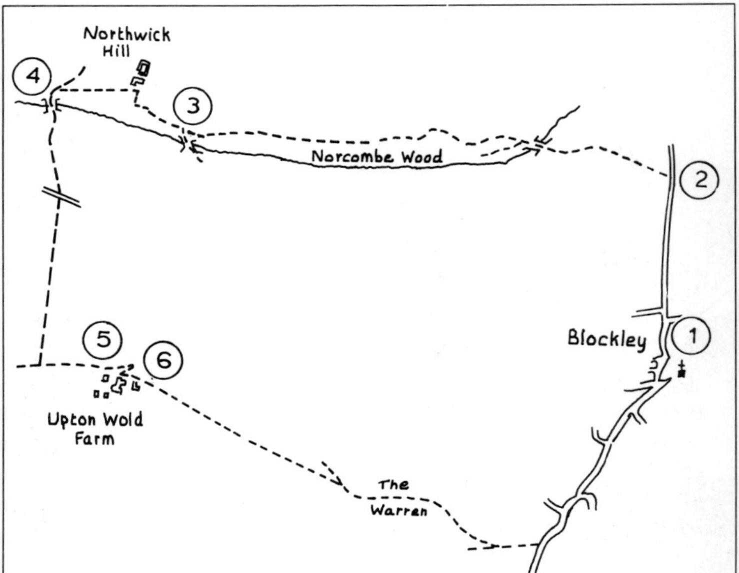

Walk up the hill with the post office (left), passing the bowling green (right) in the direction of Broad Campden. Pass St George's Hall (left) and at the end of the cottages (right) cross the road into the playing fields and follow the footpath sign diagonally right.

2. Cross the two stiles and descend the hill with large trees to the left. Aim for the wooden gate where the narrow brook passes below the pathway at the entrance to Norcombe Wood (right). Pass through the gateway, take the fork right and ascend the hill.

3. Walk ahead on the track for about 3/4 mile until a clearing is reached with a track joining left. Take about 30 paces into the clearing where there is a narrow path forking upwards (right). Follow it and pass through a gateway at the hilltop. Emerge onto a sloping field, turn left along the bottom of the game bird pens, then right towards the house ahead. At Northwick Hill turn left to join the gravel path and

Blockley's main street

continue down through the trees along the track.

4. Pass a track (left) and a notice (right) "Private No Entry". Bear left up the track leaving the woods behind with Holt Farm up left near the road. Cross the road and follow the bridleway sign ahead. Turn 90° left at the tarmac driveway and walk along it towards Upton Wold Farm.

5. As you approach the farm take the driveway which curves away left from the house. At the pillared gateway to the drive turn right, follow the drive down towards the farm house but just before you reach it turn left onto the unmarked path and walk down to the wooden gate ahead with the stone wall (right).

6. Exit via the gateway into the field, walk straight ahead, pass through a second gateway and walking close to the edge of the wood (left) aim for the bottom left corner of the field. Pass through the gateway, turn right and follow the path down through The Warren. Pass right of a large detached house set in a

Blockley. The main street looking towards the church

clearing before joining the main street of Blockley at its southern end. Turn left to walk between picturesque properties clustered close along the narrow road for 1/2 mile back to the start.

Places and Points of Interest Along the Way

BLOCKLEY

Miracles were supposed to have been performed by St Wulstan back in the ninth century at Blockley and formerly the parish was

The Church of St Peter and St Paul, Blockley

owned by King Burgred who sold it to the Bishops of Worcester for 300 shillings. Much later, during the 1600s, the silk industry, founded here by the Rushout family, flourished and brought great prosperity to the area for about 200 years. By 1824 there were 8 mills working at Blockley employing about 3,000 people including the outworkers. The power source, as with most industry of the period, was water and here it came from the stream that runs beside the High Street. Alas, like all good things, it came to an end and by 1885 the mills were used for a variety of other purposes.

The same family whose ancestors had introduced the silk trade restored the church in 1868 and after an outbreak of cholera in the area, built a sewage system and installed a piped water supply from a reservoir at nearby Dovedale. Sixteen years later the water power was used to generate electricity for their Northwick Park home and shortly after for the whole village, thus Blockley was one of the earliest villages in Britain to have electricity.

The Church of St Peter and St Paul at Blockley is a large one and reflects the village's former prosperity. It has a Norman chancel and in the fourteenth-century north aisle is the Rushout family vault. The church also contains a number of brasses.

Not far away, just past Dovedale, the Anglo-Saxon village of Upton Wold, which was abandoned at the time of the Black Death, is now being excavated.

Russell Spring, Blockley

9: Laverton, Snowshill, Stanton

Map Landranger:	150
Start:	GR: SP 075 356
Distance:	$5^{1}/_{2}$ miles

This route forms a link between the attractive village of Laverton and two of the most popular villages in the northern region of the Cotswolds, Snowshill and Stanton. The walk is quite steep and crosses some of the higher parts of the Wolds and consequently it can be quite a bleak walk in the winter months. The Mount Inn at Stanton is a good place to take refreshment en-route.

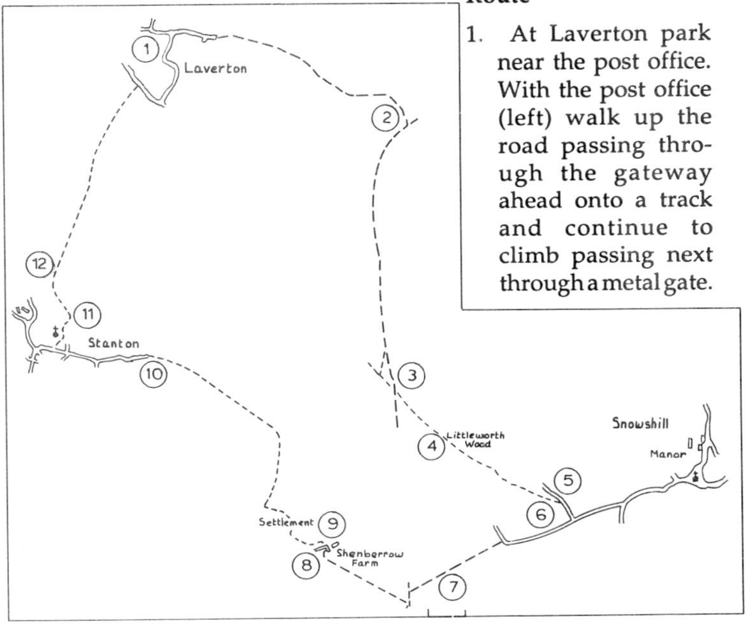

Route

1. At Laverton park near the post office. With the post office (left) walk up the road passing through the gateway ahead onto a track and continue to climb passing next through a metal gate.

The old school house, Laverton

2. Follow the track round (right), pass through a wooden gate and take the track (right) indicated by the Cotswold Way sign. Walk up the incline passing a disused quarry (left) until the summit is reached.

3. Here you are joined by a path from the right and immediately a second path from the right with the Cotswold Way sign, continue ahead and follow the pathway as it bears left passing metal gates (right) with a blue arrow marker.

4. Go down the hill, with wood (left), until the National Trust Littleworth Wood sign is reached. Go left onto the path through the wood.

5. At the tarmac lane at the bottom of the wood turn right with Snowshill village down to the left, walk to the T-junction where Snowshill can be visited by turning left. Retrace your steps to this point to continue the walk.

6. Turn right up the lane until it turns sharp right where you take the track left through the metal gate. Take the path diagonally left following the direction indicated by the blue arrow marker.

7. Part of the way up the field is a metal gateway in the stone wall, the right of way is indicated by the blue arrow marker, follow

Snowshill Manor, the south front

it to the top left of the next field, pass onto the track (left) for a short distance and pass through the first metal gate with a blue arrow marker (right) onto the track towards Shenberrow Farm.

8. At the farm turn right then left between the barns signposted Broadway. Follow the track to the T-junction. Go left at the sign Stanton 2km passing right of the rear of the farm.

9. Keeping hard right here, follow the track round and down, across the ancient "settlement" into the village of Stanton where the Mount Inn is right.

10. Walk down the village street until a crossroad is reached, turn right into the lane at Cross Cottage where the right of way passes to the right of the Church of St Michael and All Angels

Cottages at Snowshill

The forty year old tour bus regularly visits Stanton

and exits to the left of a high stone wall.

11. Before the stile turn left with a high hedge and metal fence (left) and follow the path through a metal kissing gate into a field, cross the field bearing right.

12. Follow the right of way over the fields back to the road at Laverton. Turn right then left and pass the Old School (right) to reach the post office.

Places and Points of Interest Along the Way

LAVERTON

This attractive small village is typical of this part of the Cotswolds. It is in fact little more than a T-junction of lanes, with the old school house and post office set amidst a huddle of cottages. At the head of the main street the tarmac surface runs out, developing into a track which heads up towards the hills and woods that form a most pleasant backdrop for the village.

The church of St Barnabas at Snowshill

SNOWSHILL

There is no main street as such in Snowshill where the village, seemingly lonely and exposed, clings to a steep fold in one of lower escarpments which breaks the overall contours of the higher wolds. The houses and cottages were built where there was a flat area sufficiently large to take them and must have had to be set at different levels in order to find space to squeeze them in. Surrounded by these lovely old buildings is the small Church of St Barnabas which was completely rebuilt in 1864 in a sturdy, pseudo Gothic style. Consequently, it doesn't appear to fit in so well with its surroundings as do most Cotswold village churches.

The village is dominated by the lovely sixteenth-century Manor House, now owned by the National Trust. In 1919, Charles Wade bought the house to use as a home for his collection of almost everything from dead beetles to farm carts to toys and cabinets, while he lived in the small priest's house in the garden. The manor itself has a fine Tudor interior with windows dating from about 1700.

The Manor at Snowshill

The main street, Stanton

STANTON

Sitting at the foot of the western scarp of the Cotswolds, the main street of Stanton is really the village's only street. It climbs gently between close packed cottages on each side of the road up to the Mount Inn at the top of the hill. Most of the houses here date from 1570 to 1650 but much of their traditional appearance is a result of the work of Sir Philip Stott who lived at Stanton during the period 1906-37 when restoration work was carried out.

The village Church of St Michael and All Angels was rebuilt in the fifteenth century. Inside, the nave arcade is Norman and the font dates from the fifteenth century; unusually the church has two pulpits, one is made of wood from the fourteenth century and the other is seventeenth century. At the bottom of the village is Stanton Court, built by the Izod family during the seventeenth century and much refurbished along with the rest of the village by Sir Philip Stott.

10: Long Compton, Great Rollright, Little Rollright, The Rollright Stones

Map Landranger:	151
Start:	GR: SP 291 327
Distance:	$7^{1}/_{2}$ miles

Starting in the village of Long Compton this walk continues through Great Rollright and the tiny hamlet of Little Rollright with the opportunity to visit the famous Rollright Stones. The route is hilly with some steady climbs and is for the most part across farm land with excellent views. To complete the walk and take in all the places at hand allow a full day for this route.

Route

1. On reaching Long Compton when travelling north on the A34, turn right into Butlers Lane and after passing the farm buildings (right) go left towards Weston Court. Having parked your car walk to where the lane turns sharply left. Take the track (right) and follow it for about $1^{1}/_{4}$ miles. At the top up to the left is Yardley Barn amongst the trees. Close by (left) is a metal gate, turn right and walk at right angles to the track along the bridleway with the hedge close by (right).
2. At the bottom right of the field cross the footbridge and pass through the gate with the blue arrow marker. Go into the field, turn right and walk with the hedge (right). Eventually, after a copse of trees go through a wooden fence in the hedge (right) and continue up the field.
3. Walking with trees (right) continue up the fields, passing farm buildings over to the left. At the trees ahead go through the metal gate (right), cross the top of the field and pass through the metal gate ahead. Turn left and walk up the field aiming for the marker ahead.

The picturesque old church gateway seen from the churchyard at Long Compton

4. At the top of the field pass through the metal gate, along a short distance of track then turn left through a gateway. Walk up the field and exit through a gate onto the road.

5. Cross the road and turn left on to the right of way. Follow the right of way round (right) with the wood (right) until the road is reached. Turn left then right into Great Rollright.

6. Leave the village by the same route as you entered. Turn left at the crossroads. Where the road bends right, go left onto the track turning right as it bears away from the road. Continue along the track, across the fields, until the road is reached.

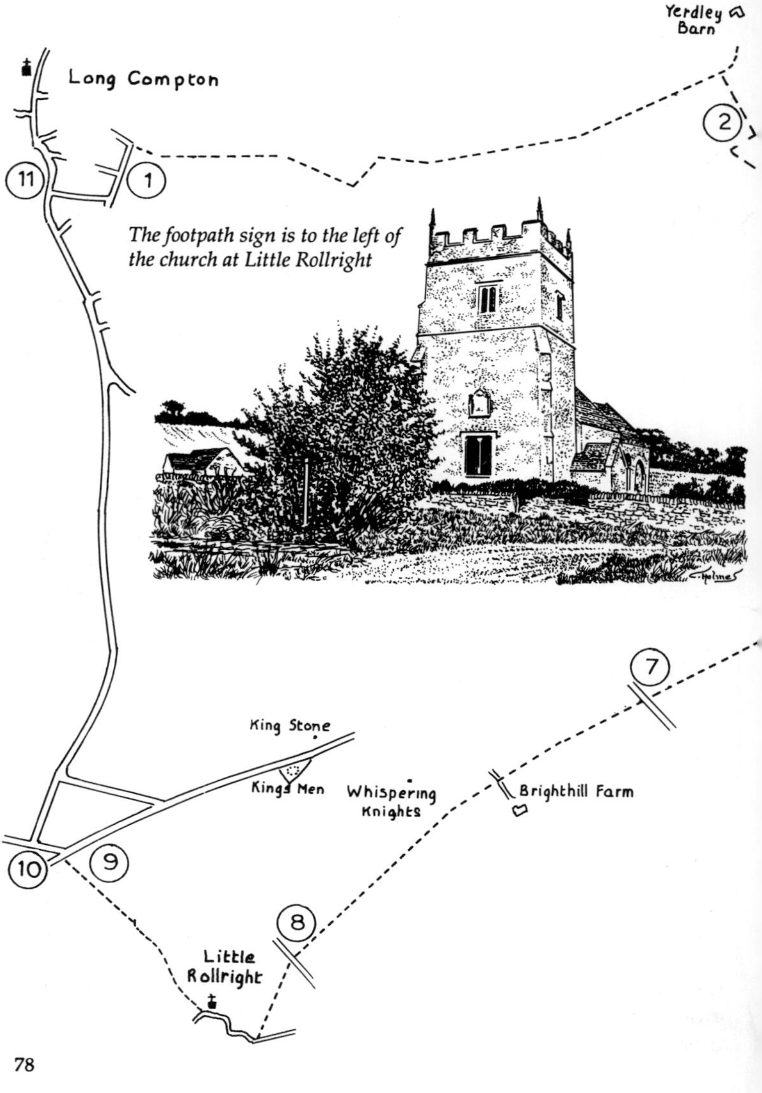

The footpath sign is to the left of the church at Little Rollright

7. Cross the road and slightly to the right is the right of way. Continue ahead passing Brighthill Farm (left) until the road above Little Rollright is revealed.

8. To visit this tiny hamlet follow the path down with the church (right) to join the lane, then walk along the lane to pass in front of the church. Follow the footpath sign to the left of the Church, climb up the hill and turn right at the field top then left and continue to the road.

9. To visit the Rollright Stones turn right and walk along the road. After your visit return to the crossroads with the Toll Cottage (left). Turn right and follow the road to Long Compton.

10. If you don't wish to visit the Rollright Stones take the road ahead of you, then go first right and walk along the road to Long Compton.

11. As you return to the village turn right into Butlers Lane and after passing the farm buildings (right), go left towards Weston Court.

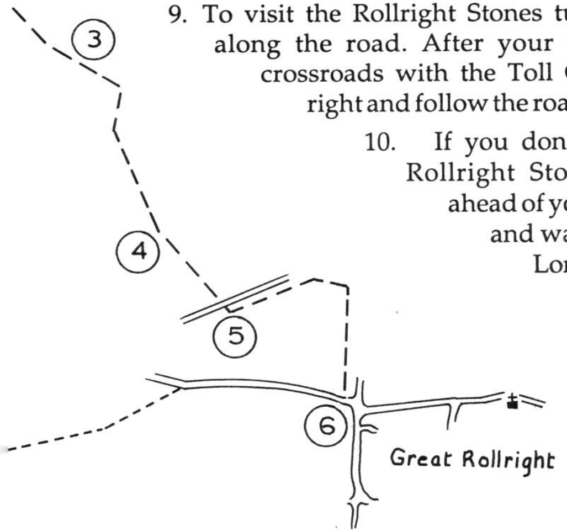

Places and Points of Interest Along the Way

LITTLE ROLLRIGHT

The tiny, picturesque hamlet of Little Rollright stands in its own valley and consists of a couple of farm buildings, the small Church of St Philip and the former rectory. The church, probably built by local monks, combines a fourteenth-century chancel, a fifteenth-century nave and a tower dated 1617. It contains two very large canopied tombs. One is an effigy of a recumbent knight in full plate armour with a shield emblazoned with the arms of the Dixon family who were Lords of the Manor; the other has a group of three effigies around a prayer desk. The Elizabethan chalice, dated 1571, is still used.

In 1086 the village was home to around ninety persons but by 1284 only five people were recorded as being resident here. It is felt that due to the land enclosures the majority of people were evicted from their land in order to turn it into sheep pastures. The remains of the former village is thought to be to the north of the church.

ROLLRIGHT STONES

The Rollright Stones is a prehistoric stone circle set on a 700ft high ridge just north of Chipping Norton. Its age is not really known but informed opinion puts it at about 3,500 years.

The King's Men consists of about seventy pitted, weather beaten uprights set in a circle of approximately 100ft diameter. Further across the field five upright stones, known as the Whispering Knights, are thought to indicate a burial chamber. Across the road and over the county boundary in Warwickshire stands the strangely shaped 8ft high King Stone apparently standing watch over the slope towards the village of Long Compton.

The King Stone, Rollright

Over the centuries many legends have grown up around these stones. One such legend has it that in days gone by a certain King was intent on conquering England and he met a witch. The witch turned the King and his men into stone, then she did likewise to his knights who were plotting and whispering together. Through the ages local folk held these stones in awe. It is said that one farmer ignored the superstitions and tried to remove one stone with a team of horses. At the end of the day he had succeeded in moving it only a few yards; thus convinced of the power of the stone he felt he ought to put it back where it belonged. This he did with ease with the help of a single horse.

The Whispering Knights

11: Oxenton Hill

Map Landranger:	150
Start:	GR: SO 964 330
Distance:	$8^1/_2$ miles

This circular, undulating walk around Oxenton Hill links the tiny hamlets of Teddington, Oxenton, Woolstone and Alstone, and provides the walker with wonderful views across the surrounding valleys to the wooded hills beyond.

It is one of the few publess routes among these walks and therefore walkers will need to carry their own refreshments.

On leaving Teddington village walk with the fence on the left

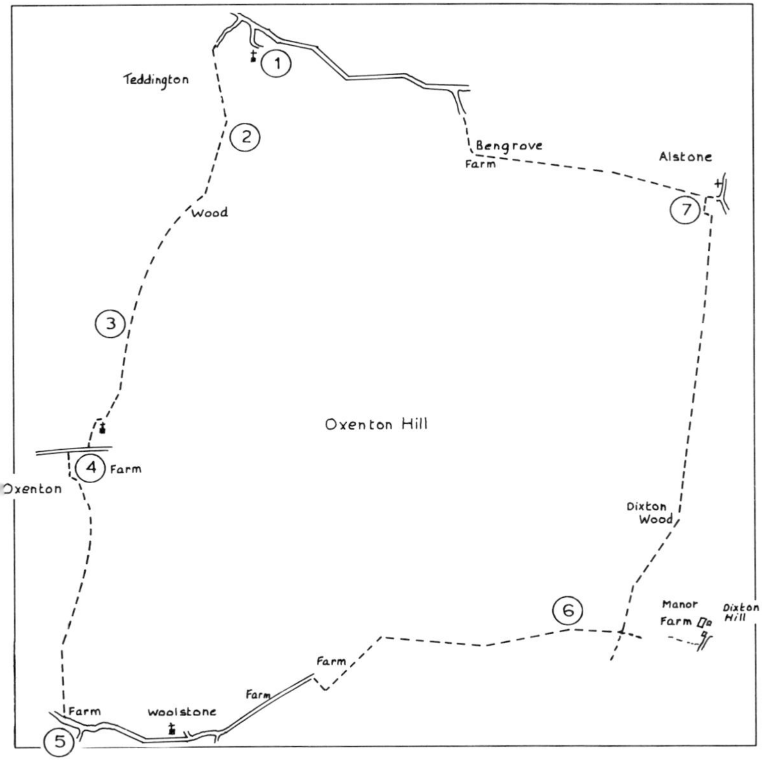

Route

1. Park near the church at Teddington. Walk down the lane passing the post box (right) to join the main street. Turn left pass the cottage called Overton (left) and take the next turning left. Walk down the track between the buildings of Box Tree Farm, cross the stile by the gate with the yellow arrow marker and walk up the hill close to the fence (left).

2. Cross the next stile and continue up the hill keeping the fence (left). Go over the next stile and bearing right follow the arrow markers through the wood. Emerging from the wood, walk

The church at Oxenton

along the edge of the field as it slopes down right, until you reach a stile, marked with a yellow marker, at the corner of a wire fence (right).

3. Cross into the field and walk slightly to the right in the direction of Oxenton church which is ahead amongst the trees. Cross a further stile lower down the slope before reaching the church. Pass through the churchyard, turn right at the road and take the track (left) beside the buildings of Field Farm.

4. Pass through the wooden gate with the yellow arrow marker (left) then continue ahead, crossing the fields by way of the stiles, the third of which is diagonally (right) in the fence ahead next to a large tree stump. Walk diagonally right to cross the next stile in the wire fence (right). Turn sharp left, pass through the metal gate and turn diagonally right aiming for the bottom corner (right) of the field. Pass the farm buildings, cross the stile and take the footbridge ahead (left) onto the road.
5. Turn left, pass Grange Farm (left) and follow the road in the direction of Woolstone passing Grove Hill Farm (left). At Woolstone Hill Farm turn right just before the metal buildings to gain access via the metal gate to the bridleway on the right side. Walk ahead up the hill, at the top of which turn right following the track over the fields.
6. With Dixton Hill as a backcloth for Manor Farm, pass through a hedge by way of a gate on the bridleway or a stile (right), then watch for a further stile over to the right on the footpath that crosses the bridleway, here you should turn left and climb up the hill to the left side of the wire fence enclosing a copse. Cross the yellow arrow marked stile and with Dixton Wood (left)

Dixton Hill

The tiny and unusual Church of St Margaret's at Alstone

walk diagonally (right) down the field aiming for the stile in the hedge close to the road (right). Pass a barn (left) cross two more stiles and aim for the bottom left corner of the field where the buildings of Alstone are visible ahead. Go over the stile, turn right and pass a modern house called Two Hoots. Turn right again if you wish to visit the village.

7. To continue the walk retrace your steps to the footpath, walk ahead across the fields following the yellow arrow markers with the hedge (left) until a stile in the hedge ahead is revealed; cross it and walk straight ahead to the farm at Bengrove. Follow the track round (right) to the wood. Turn left and follow the lane to return to Teddington.

Places and Points of Interest Along the Way

Teddington gives very much the impression of being a dormitory village with recent housing development and little else. The Church of St Nicholas, however, dates from much earlier times and its high, stilted, semi-circular chancel arch is said to be of Anglo-Saxon

Leaving Alstone behind we walk across the fields towards Teddington

inspired design, similar to those at Deerhurst (Walk 15), and is probably eleventh or twelfth century. The nave is probably thirteenth century, the chancel itself fourteenth century and the tower about 100 years younger again. The east end of the tower vault has a pair of clustered columns dating from the thirteenth century which it is thought may have come from Hailes Abbey (Walk 12) after the dissolution of the monasteries. On the south wall of the nave is a painting of the coat of arms of William and Mary with a rather crude architectural framework.

At tiny Oxenton there is very little recent development and old houses mingle well with church and farm buildings alike. A pair of Flemish or German fifteenth-century armour clad men were stolen from the chancel of St John the Baptist Church at Oxenton and those in position today are replicas made in 1980. Otherwise the church, which belonged to Tewkesbury Abbey until the dissolution of the monasteries, is almost perfect for a thirteenth-century place of worship. Much restoration was carefully carried out during the early 1900s but the roof of the north aisle still retains its original oak beams and some of the original paintings are still visible on the north and west walls.

The village school at Oxenton was founded, in 1847 by the Earl of Ellenborough, a large landowner locally who held high offices in the state, particularly in India. He is buried at Oxenton. The school was closed in 1907 and since 1924 has served as the village hall.

Woolstone consists of three farms and a sprinkling of picturesque dwellings along the main street. Behind a small brick and timber frame barn is the Church of St Martin De Tours. More modern than the previous two churches, it was restored and partially re-built in 1499 and again in 1873. The original church could have been Saxon for it was attached to Deerhurst Priory as early as 1271, also the priest's chair of rough black oak dates from about 1640 and could have been made from an old communion table as at Deerhurst. From ancient times Woolstone belonged to the Diocese of Worcester until it was transferred to the See of Gloucester in 1541 by Henry VIII.

Down on the flatland again, at the foot of the hill, sits Alstone on a bend in the lane. It is a little larger than the previous two hamlets but not much. Alstone has some recent development but older properties as well. The part stone and part timber frame buildings of Manor Farm are particularly attractive and quite unusual as is the eighteenth-century rectangular timber bell tower atop the thirteenth-century Church of St Margaret's.

12: Stanway, Wood Stanway, Hailes, Didbrook

Map Landranger:	150
Start:	GR: SP 061 326
Distance:	$5^{1}/_{2}$ miles

This route consists of three sections, the first from Stanway to Wood Stanway is level and uses tarmac and footpath. The second section from Wood Stanway is along the footpaths and tracks of the Cotswold Way and it is quite steep and wooded but there are some good views as you drop down towards Hailes with its interesting Abbey remains. The return from here to Stanway is level and on footpaths across fields.

The thatched cricket pavilion at Stanway

Route

1. After passing the entrance to Stanway House (right) follow the road round (right) and park the car on the verge by the stile (right) where the sign reads Stanton 2km and Cotswold Way. Walk back towards Stanway House with the thatched cricket pavilion (right). Pass the Church and then the entrance to Stanway House (left). Take the track (left), the notice reads Stanway Estate Yard.
2. Pass the cottage (right), bear left passing the Cotswold Way sign, go through the wooden kissing gate with the swan's head carved on it. Follow the arrows to the road. Turn left, cross the road and take the path (right) at the Cotswold Way sign.
3. Follow the yellow arrow markers across the fields exiting through a metal gate onto the road.
4. Turn right then left at the signpost Hailes Abbey 2km. Follow the lane round (right), past Keepers Cottage (left), past the old water faucet (left), then through the metal gate, between the cottages ahead and turn left. Look for the

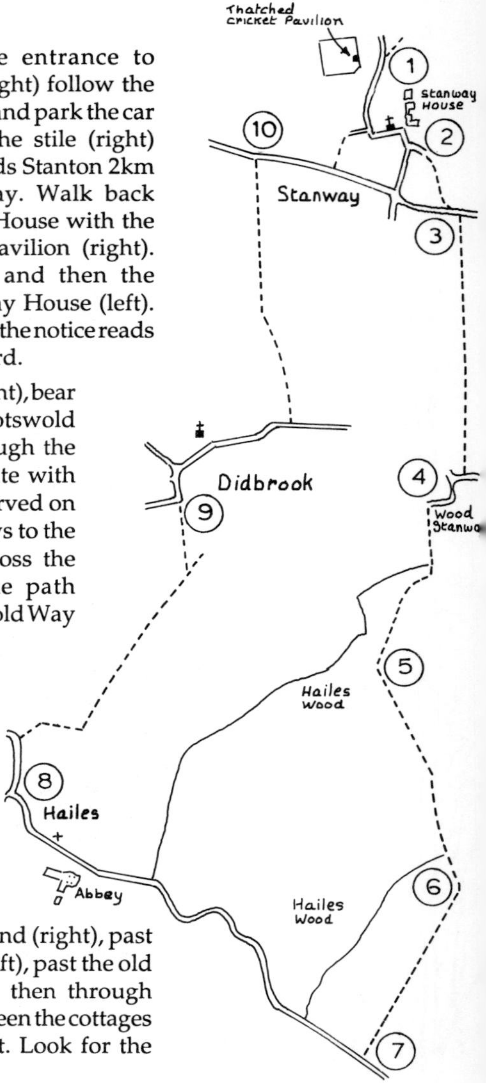

yellow arrow marker up on the gateway ahead to left of the wood as you start your ascent of the hill. Go through the gate and follow close to the wood (right). As the trees ahead are approached aim for the top left of the field where the wire fence (left) meets the trees.

5. Cross the stile and follow the yellow arrow markers as you climb up the hill, keeping Hailes Wood close by (right). When the end of the wood is reached cross the stile (right) and walk close to the wire fence (left).

6. At the arrow marker ahead, to the left of which is a group of about a dozen trees, swing diagonally right and ahead is a fence with a gate in it. Go through the gate then straight ahead to start the descent of the track at the signpost ahead.

7. Turn right at the Bridleway and follow it towards Hailes Abbey. At the bottom of the hill join the tarmac lane with the fruit farm (left) and continue along the roadway to the Abbey ruins (left) and the twelfth-century church (right).

8. Continue to follow the road as it bears right then left and at the junction go right where the road curves

The fifteenth century seal from Hailes Abbey

to the left then right onto the track at the signpost reading Stanway 3km. At the junction turn left and follow the markers through the fields for about 3/8 mile to a stile ahead. To the left of the stile is a large tree, turn left and in the hedge to the left of the tree is a stile with a yellow arrow marker, cross it and go diagonally (right) aiming for the gate ahead with the telephone box beyond.

9. Pass through the gate, turn right through Didbrook. Pass the church (left) and after the bend in the road, just before the wood (left) turn left over a stile onto a footpath. Follow the arrow markers across the fields with a hedge (left), all the way back to the B4077 road.

The gatehouse to the Manor at Stanway

10. At the road turn right and just before the road sign to Stanway go left over the stile. Walk down the slope and cross the brook by a footbridge and stile, then follow the path (right) and enter the village, between the cottages with the church ahead. Turn left and retrace your steps back to the car.

Places and Points of Interest Along the Way

STANWAY

Church, tithe-barn and manor stand side by side at Stanway, seemingly closely related though in fact hundreds of years divide them. The handsome barn is six centuries old and was once owned by the Abbey of Tewkesbury. The church is fourteenth century and the Manor, with its quite magnificent renaissance style gate-house attributed to Inigo Jones is more "modern", being sixteenth century. The cottages that make up the village are no less appealing albeit in a more humble way.

In its heyday this was a busy place with a cider mill, corn mill, fulling mill and later a mill for paper making, but it is not so busy today. How time has changed all that!

In 1921 Sir James Barrie, the creator of *Peter Pan* (and bequeather of all the royalties thereof to the Great Ormond Street Childrens' Hospital) became associated with the village. He rented Stanway House and in 1924 presented the village cricket club with a new pavilion to replace the old railway coach which had been used previously. The new pavilion was made of timber, had a thatched roof and was supported on staddle feet and is still used today.

It is said that Barrie's bedroom at Stanway House looked out onto the church and lying in bed one morning a dancing image of the sun reflecting off the church's golden weather vane gave him the inspiration for Tinkerbell, the fairy in *Peter Pan*. The fact that the play was first produced in 1904 and published as a novel in 1911 must, however, discount the tale.

Another resident, during the house's earlier history was Thomas Dover, the grandson of Dr Robert Dover who was attributed during his privateering days with the rescue of Alexander Selkirk, the "Robinson Crusoe" from the Pacific island of Juan Fernandez. The same privateer is the acknowledged developer of mercury based medicines, becoming known as the "Quicksilver Doctor" during

Hailes Church

the early 1700s.

HAILES ABBEY and HAILES CHURCH

It would seem that the younger brother of Henry III, Richard, Earl

Hailes Abbey

of Cornwall was almost certainly about to be shipwrecked when his luck changed and he lived to tell the tale. As a result of this experience in 1245 he founded the Abbey for the Cistercian monks as an act of thanksgiving. Richard's second son, Edmund, presented a phial of "Christ's Blood" to the Abbey in 1270 and a new shrine with five radiating chapels was built to house the valuable new treasure. As a result it became one of the great centres in England for pilgrims and at its peak of popularity around 13,000 acres of land were owned by the Abbey, however, on Christmas Eve 1539 came its dissolution; the roofing lead, ornaments, valuables and all its plate were stripped. Today only parts of the cloister arches remain as an indication of its former splendour. With its close mown lawns and fine trees in its tranquil setting, it has a beauty all of its own.

When the Abbey was founded the Hailes church was already about 100 years old but its structure was modified during the fourteenth century. Its tiny, half-timbered tower is quite a rarity and inside it has panels of mediaeval stained glass and wall paintings, a fifteenth-century rood screen and seventeenth-century furnishings are amongst its rich and varied interior.

DIDBROOK

Perhaps the most unusual thing about Didbrook are some cottages in the village which are partly constructed of the traditional Cotswold stone and partly of a timber frame type construction, giving a similar appearance to some of the older buildings at the centre of Northleach. The "black and white" appearance certainly adds to the charm of the village, with numbers 62 and 63 being of the old "cruck" type construction.

The church, St George's, was rebuilt in 1475 by Abbot Whitchurch of Hailes. It is generally assumed that the decision to rebuild was taken as the existing church was the scene of the murder of Lancastrian "refugees" from Tewksbury. The church's tower is quite unique in that it is supported within the nave by three open arches

13: Longborough, Donnington

Map Landranger:	163
Start:	GR: SP 178 293
Distance:	2½ miles

This is a pleasant, short walk over undulating terrain which affords fine views across typical high wold countryside. Today, the small hamlet of Donnington consists mainly of the manor and its subsidiary buildings, but during the English Civil War the surrounding countryside was the scene of much fighting. At Longborough, with its attractive honey coloured buildings, you will find the Coach and Horses Inn which is a fine example of village hostelry.

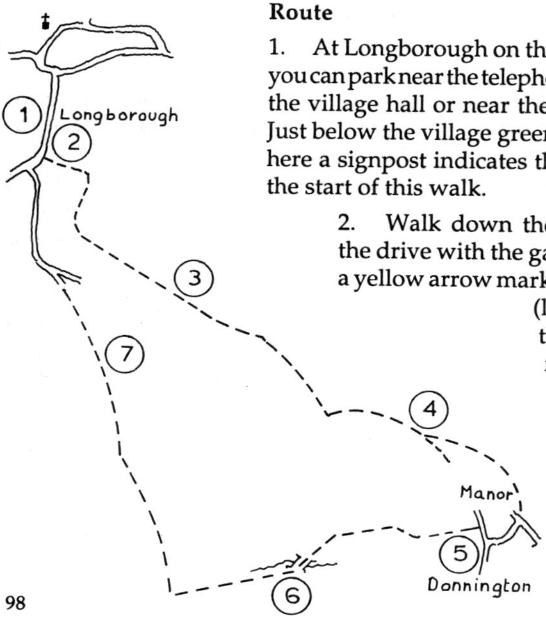

Route

1. At Longborough on the road to Stow, you can park near the telephone box outside the village hall or near the village green. Just below the village green is small pool, here a signpost indicates the footpath for the start of this walk.

2. Walk down the right side of the drive with the garage (left) and a yellow arrow marker on the fence (left). Go down the path into the field with a high hedge (right). Cross the stile (right), follow the path to cross three further stiles turning

The stone dog at Donnington Hall

left into the field. Walk with a hedge close (left) until the hedge at the corner (left) is reached, then head diagonally over the field towards the yellow arrow marker on the opposite side.

3. Walk close to the hedge (right) until a wooden gate with a blue arrow marker is reached. Pass through the gate, turn left and walk down the track passing through the next two blue arrow marked gates ahead onto a path with woods (left) and wire fence (right). At the top of the wood, follow the path left 90° continuing with the fence (right), passing through the next blue arrow marked gate and walk diagonally right up the field, through the next gate and as Donnington Manor is approached fork left.

4. Skirting round the farm buildings, pass through a metal gate, then go over a stile and with the manor (right) pass through a metal gate into the lane where the signpost says Longborough and indicates a bridleway. Walk ahead between the cottages passing the former forge (left) now a cottage, and at the T-junction turn right onto a track.

5. At the water pump (left) go through the metal gate into the field. Walk with a stone wall (left), cross the stile then aim diagonally right to the gate at the right end of the stone wall ahead. Pass through the gate, walk ahead with high hedges (right), cross the stile at the field top then drop down diagonally left towards the tree in the hedge ahead. Cross the footbridge and stile then turn right.

At the water pump go through the metal gate on the left

6. Aim for the left corner of the woods ahead. Cross the stile, turn immediately right, go over the second stile, then straight ahead down the field crossing the footbridge with the woods over to the right. Exit from the bottom of the field over a footbridge in the trees. Go left over the stile and walk ahead with the wooden fence (right).

7. After the next stile the fence is left. Cross two more stiles and join the track ahead at the blue arrow marker. Follow the track round (right) to the end of Love Walk then along the lane into the village.

Places and Points of Interest Along the Way

LONGBOROUGH

The small, attractive village of Longborough sits more or less at a T-junction of the roads on a hillside overlooking the Evenlode Valley: a typical Cotswold conglomeration of 300 year old cottages and farm buildings, with the inn and the church at its centre.

Three manors formed the village which consisted of around fifty families at the time of the Domesday Book. Banks Fee, to the south

The small pool near the village green, Longborough

Longborough village

of the village, one of the three, can still be identified. In 1246 Henry III 'gave' Longborough to his brother Richard, Earl of Cornwall, who founded Hailes Abbey (Walk 12). Later, in 1301, his son Edmund made a present of it to Hailes. In 1554 the manor of Longborough was granted to Sir Roland Hill, former Lord Mayor of London. His colleague, Sir Thomas Leigh also acquired Adlestrop and Stoneleigh Manors. Eventually all three manors came into the possession of the Leigh family.

The original Church of St James was constructed with a simple knave and chancel during the twelfth century and 100 years later the tower was added. The church's finest feature is the lovely fourteenth-century transept with the very large decorated window.

The road through Donnington

A fourteenth-century knight lies here, as does Sir William Leigh in his splendid black and white marble tomb dating from 1631.

DONNINGTON

At Donnington there is little else besides the Grand Hall and the subsidiary out buildings that supported it over the generations. Yet Donnington has a most famous place in English history, for it was here in 1646 that the elderly Lord Astley surrendered his army to Cromwell's army. His words before the Battle of Newbury are well recorded:

> "Lord I shall be verie busie this day
> I may forget Thee, but doe not Thou forget me!"

He was on his way to Oxford to join the King but was taken as he neared Stow and surrendered, a tired old man, to the Parliamentarians.

14: Winchcombe, Belas Knap, Sudeley Castle

Map Landranger:	163
Start:	GR: SP 024 284
Distance:	5 miles

This route climbs gradually from Winchcombe up to Belas Knap and on the descent to Sudeley Castle there are panoramic views of Winchcombe and the surrounding countryside. The walk is suitable for all weather conditions.

Route

1. Park in the long stay car park at Winchcombe and exit to the main street via Cowl Lane. Turn right, passing the Plasterers Alms (left) then walk into Vine Street, (left), signposted Cotswold Way and Sudeley Castle.
2. Immediately after crossing the bridge take the path (right) through the metal kissing gate and with the river (right) walk along the path crossing the stiles until the road is reached. Turn left and continue until the signpost which reads Belas Knap $1^{1}/_{2}$ miles (right).
3. Leave the road and follow the track for

The entrance to Belas Knap

1/4 mile until a stile (left) is reached, cross it and follow the signs up the hill. Go over one more stile before reaching the field top, then cross a stone stile onto the road.

4. Walk up the road straight ahead signposted Belas Knap. Take the next path (right). Go over the stile and climb the 1km to Belas Knap.
5. Retrace your steps to the road, turn right. At the Cotswold Way sign go left down the track with cottages (right). Pass to the right of the farm buildings and take the indicated path with the metal fence (left) and Sudeley Castle over to the right.
6. At the bottom of the hill cross a small footbridge and with the old gatehouse to the castle (right) continue ahead into Winchcombe.

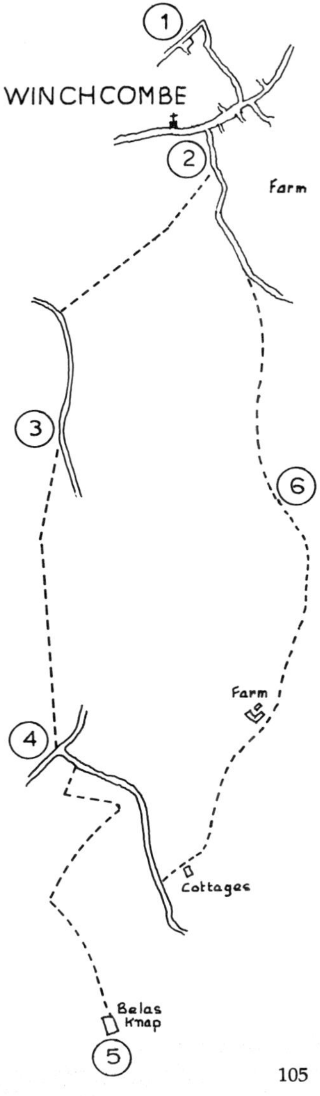

Places and Points of Interest Along the Way

WINCHCOMBE

Kenulf, King of Mercia, founded a Benedictine Abbey at Winchcombe in AD 798. The king's son, Kenelm, was buried in the abbey following his murder and as a consequence of this the Abbey became a place of pilgrimage for believers over the following years. The Abbey was destroyed in 1539 by Lord Seymour

The track up to Belas Knap

after the dissolution of the monasteries but two stone coffins, said to be those of the Mercian King and his son, survived and are now in Winchcombe church.

Much later the Civil War raged around the town, as it did in many other parts of the Cotswolds, indeed the Church of St Peter's still bears the marks, chiefly on the tower, of shot and shrapnel from those days. The church was built about 1465 and the forty-five exterior gargoyles are said to be of notable people of the period, a

Walk down the hill with the metal fence on the left

fairly common practice at that time. Inside the church is light and airy, having clerestory windows of pale green glass on each side. On the north wall is a fourteenth-century altar cloth, originally thought to be the work of Catherine of Aragon.

Across Queen Square is Jacobean House. Originally constructed in the early 1600s and thought to be the work of Inigo Jones, it was extensively rebuilt some 250 years later. The Chandos family were the Lords of the Manor during the Elizabethan period and they had the almshouses built nearby in 1573.

The River Isbourne flows quite close and is reached from Queen Square via Duck Street where the women suspected of witchcraft were ducked. Nowadays Duck Street, the site of a number of attractive cottages, is known as Vine Street. Linked with the same period are the old stocks outside the Town Hall that houses the local history museum. Opposite is the George Inn that dates from the sixteenth century and used to be a hostel for pilgrims visiting Kenulf's Abbey.

It is not generally known that Winchcombe had much to do with the early production of tobacco in this country. Rumour has it that it was introduced to the area by Sir Walter Raleigh who was reputed

The Jacobean House in Queen's Square, Winchcombe

to have lived at Brockhampton at one time. Around 1620 a fellow by the name of John Stratford started to grow tobacco plants on about 100 acres of local land, including land at Hailes Abbey and Postlip. However, the government soon made the growing of tobacco illegal in England. Despite this, tobacco production around Winchcombe continued until about 1690. During the years between 1627 to 1652

Sudeley Castle

repeated efforts had been made to stamp out Winchcombe's tobacco growing and during 1650 riots occurred. Troops from Gloucester were sent in but were driven off by the growers and for many years these confrontations were referred to as the Tobacco Riots. After 1690 it became unprofitable to grow tobacco at Winchcombe as it was imported from America on a regular basis and this caused the price to drop. The only reminder of this part of Winchcombe's history remaining today is a street known as Tobacco Close.

SUDELEY CASTLE

The earliest parts of the present building date back to the fifteenth century when Baron Sudeley rebuilt the castle on the site of an earlier structure. During the War of the Roses the castle surrendered and passed into the hands of Edward IV.

During its history a number of famous people are reputed to have stayed here. They include Henry VIII, Anne Boleyn and Catherine of Aragon. Catherine Parr, who is buried in the castle church lived here from 1547-8 and as children so did Elizabeth I and Queen Mary. Much damage was inflicted on the castle by the Parliamentarians during the Civil War and when it was recaptured by Charles I he had his headquarters there. More recently the old chapel in the grounds, St Mary's, was restored by Gilbert Scott, the interior being entirely Victorian. The house itself accommodates a large collection of paintings, toys, dolls, tapestries and needlework.

Not far from Sudeley Castle is Belas Knap, one of the better preserved Cotswold Stone Age burial chambers where much of the dry stone walling is original. This 180ft long mound is around 4,000 years old and has entrances of "crawl through" dimensions together with a large, but false, entrance to the north. It is thought that this could have been intended to confuse evil spirits as to the position of those buried inside, or it may have been built for the purpose of confusing grave robbers. Opened in the 1860s, thirty-eight skeletons were found here together with some Roman remains.

15: Apperley, Haw Bridge, Deerhurst

Map Landranger:	150
Start:	GR: SO 862 282
Distance:	8 miles

There are two pubs along the route which is mainly on towpaths and footpaths of Coome Hill Canal and the River Severn. Deerhurst with the history steeped Odda's Chapel and the Priory adds an interesting dimension to a walk that is refreshingly different from other Cotswold walks.

Route

1. At Apperley park near the Holy Trinity Church close by the village green. Walk south in the direction of Tirley and Gloucester with the Pink Cottage (left) and the duck pond (right). At the bend in the road take the bridle path (left) following it down to the main road. Cross the road, continue

Odda's Chapel

ahead passing the timber-framed building of Mumfords Farm (left). At the bottom of the track turn left, follow the path between the trees until Coome Hill Canal is reached. Cross the bridge and turn right along the old towpath.

2. Walk along the towpath until your reach the road in about $1^{3}/_{4}$ miles. Turn left, cross the bridge over the canal and go over the stile where the signpost (right) indicates the Severn Way. Follow the footpath around to walk along the bank with the River Severn (left), to Haw Bridge about 1 mile distant.

3. As Haw Bridge is approached, pass in front of the Bridge

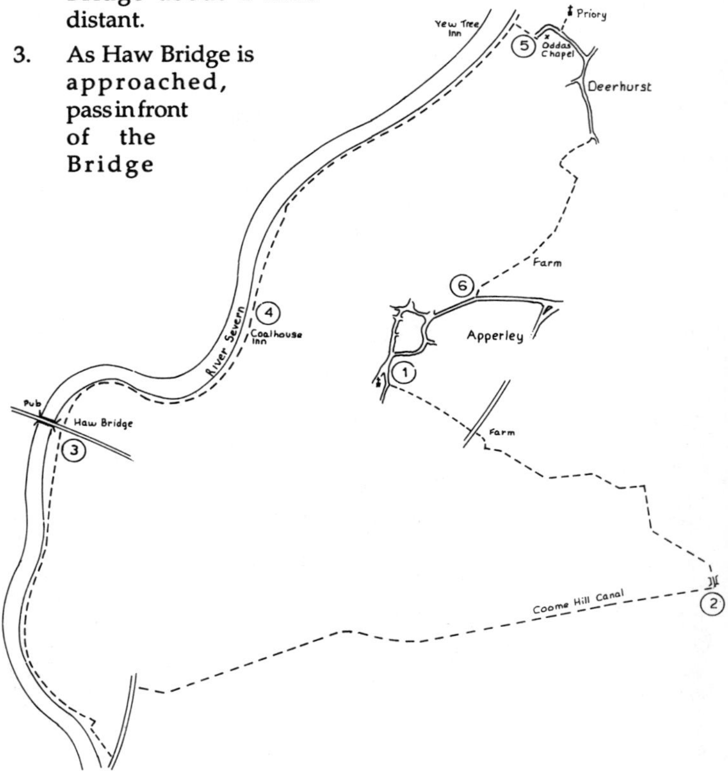

The Priory Church of St Mary, Deerhurst

House (right), cross the road with the bridge (left), go over the stile and rejoin the Severn Way ahead. Continue along the path through the caravan site to pass the Coalhouse Inn (right).

4. On passing Coalhouse Inn, go through the metal gate ahead. Follow the right of way, which is well arrow marked with yellow arrows, over the stiles until after passing the Yew Tree Inn, across the river, a large tree is reached. Turn right leaving the Severn Way Path and walk towards Odda's Chapel, just visible amongst the trees (right).

5. Pass the chapel (right) follow the lane round to pass the Priory

Church of St Mary at Deerhurst (left). Continue along the lane to the road junction. Turn right in the direction of Apperley. Go left at the next junction, walk up the "No Through Road" and where the lane bears left take the track (right). At the top turn right, follow the track across the fields with the vicarage (right). Continue over the fields and at the metal barns take the diagonal right as indicated by the arrow marker and walk towards the large tree ahead, passing the re-creational ground (left).

6. On reaching a footbridge (left), cross it, go over the recreation

Haw Bridge

The rough masonry and huge timbers inside Odda's Chapel

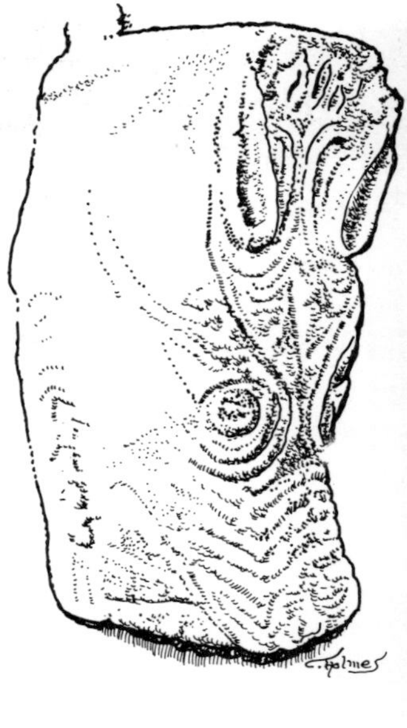

One of a pair of animal headed label Stops from the middle doorway of St Mary's church, Deerhurst

ground and at the road turn right. Follow the road to the cross roads, turn left, pass the school (left) to return to the church.

Places and Points of Interest Along the Way

COOME CANAL

Coome Canal was constructed in 1796 to transport coal from the Forest of Dean up the River Severn and on to Cheltenham. Eighty years later though, the development of the railway network proved too great a competition and the canal was forced to close. Nowadays the old canal and much of the surrounding flatland is designated as an area of special scientific interest and it was acquired by the Gloucester Trust for Nature Conservation in 1985.

DEERHURST PRIORY and ODDA'S CHAPEL

During Saxon times Deerhurst was much more important that it appears today due to the existence of its Priory. In 1016 King Canute met King Edmund here to sign a treaty redefining the boundaries dividing the lands of the Danes from the Saxon lands. The Priory at Deerhurst, thought to have been founded in the seventh century, would have ascended to even greater religious significance had it not been for the growth of the Abbeys at Gloucester and Tewksbury. During the dissolution of the monasteries it was sold off, the church being modified for use by the parish as a result of which it is claimed to be the oldest church in England. The nave is the original centre of the building with much evidence of additional interior work at different stages throughout history. The Saxon font is claimed to be the finest in this part of England.

Discovered in 1885, within the building of the house of which it is part, is Odda's Chapel. Dated 1056 it is quite small and consists of a lofty knave and tiny rough chancel. The chapel was erected to the memory of the brother of the Earl Odda who was a companion of Edward the Confessor.

16: Cleeve Hill

Map Landranger:	163
Start:	GR: SO 986 269
Distance:	$3^{1}/_{2}$ miles

I have included this walk purely because it crosses terrain that is quite unique now in the Cotswolds. The climb up from the car park is not difficult and once up there the walk is similar to walking across open moorland, it is in fact the wolds as they were many years ago before the Enclosures Act.

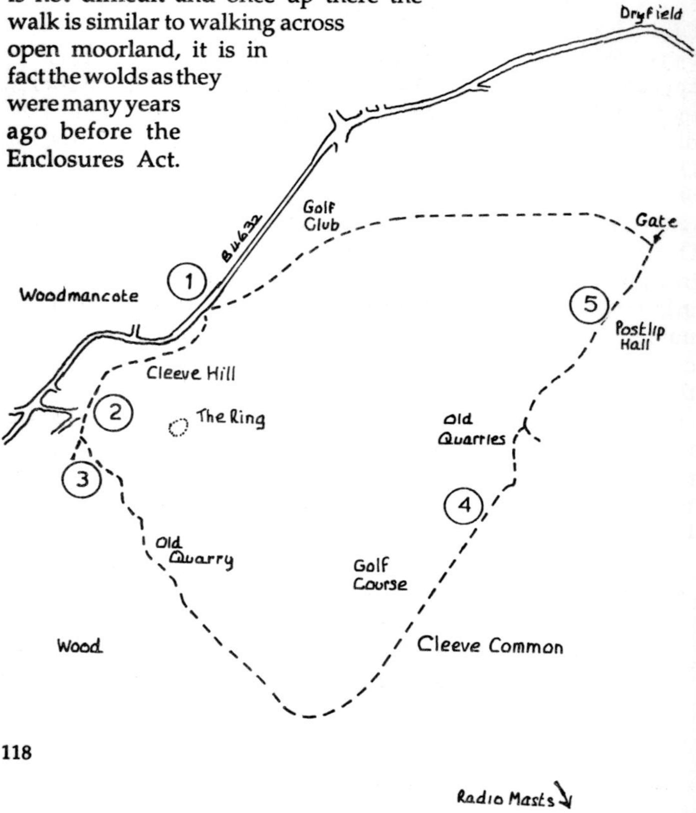

Cleeve Hill. The start of the walk with the youth hostel down to the right

The whole area is unenclosed land, so there is no danger of trespass which is just as well as the pathway signs are few and far between. The route followed is round the edge of the hill rather than across the golf course and it offers good views over Winchcombe to the north-east and to the Malvern Hills and beyond to Wales in the west.

Route

1. Park at Stockwell Lane car park which is right when travelling from Winchcombe towards Cheltenham on the A46. Just across the A46, facing Stockwell Lane is the start of entrance to the walk. Cross over the stile, turn right and walk, with the road (right), bearing left up the hill away from the road and pass behind Cleeve Hill YHA.
2. Turn left at the "No Entry Except For Access" sign which is near the junction of several paths. Follow the track passing Cleeve Scarp Rottweilers cottage down (right). Stay on the track and at the next junction, go left and walk towards the escarpment ahead.

Winchcombe in the distance seen from the old quarry workings on Cleeve Hill

Pass Cleeve Scarp Rotteweilers cottage down to the right

3. Down (right), in the distance, is Cheltenham Racecourse. At the top of the escarpment follow the track (left) until it appears that the hill top is almost reached. With the radio masts ahead (right) bear to the left away from the large white Cleeve Hill Common regulations sign which is down to the right.
4. Walk ahead, then go down the path through the old quarry workings. Follow the signs until a copse is seen ahead. Shortly the path goes down past a sign to the Cotswold Way (left). With a stile ahead, turn left up the track with a dry stone wall (right).
5. Postlip Hall is down (right). Gradually bear left away from the dry stone wall. Follow the track up to a metal gate in a wall. Go through the gate and walk ahead eventually passing the golf club house and riding stables (right). Pass to the right of the next house, cross the drive and exit onto the main road.

Places and Points of Interest Along the Way

CLEEVE HILL

At about 1,080ft in height, its summit marked by a triangular beacon, Cleeve Hill is the highest point in the Cotswold's Area of Outstanding Natural Beauty and is the last unenclosed area of the high wold left.

Despite the radiomasts, fine views from almost everywhere around the gentle slopes of the hill provide an indication of the original flow of the land in days gone by, before it was divided up by the dry stone walls forming the boundaries of farming and grazing land. It is, in fact, something akin to moorland, the only encroachment being made by the golf course.

Prehistory abounded in the immediate vicinity. The Ring, and ancient ritual circle, was surrounded by ditches, and could date from an earlier time than those built of upright stones. An Iron Age fort is just to the south as is the rough craggy Huddlestones Rock, whilst a few miles east is Belas Knap.

17: Chipping Norton, Old Chalford

Map Landranger:	164
Start:	GR: SP 314 271
Distance:	$5^3/_4$ miles

From its humble source, close to Chipping Norton, the River Glyme eventually reaches Blenheim Palace where it feeds the lake built by Capability Brown. Starting at Chipping Norton, this route follows close by the upper reaches of this rather insignificant river and passes through rolling farmland in an area of the little known Eastern Cotswolds. Choose a dry period in spring, autumn or winter when the fine views from the old road, Cow Ditch Lane, are not hidden by heavy foliage.

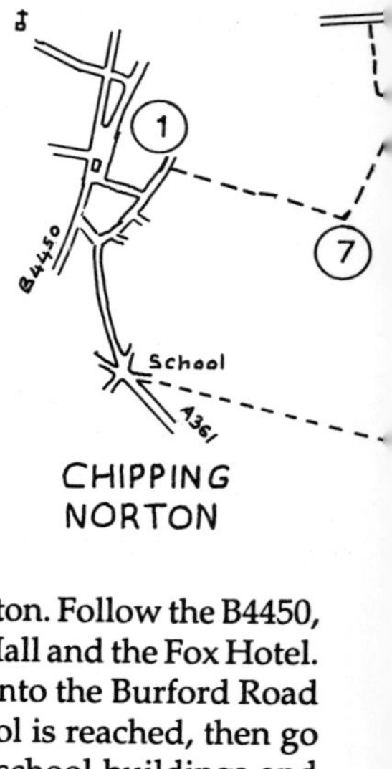

Route

1. Park in the town centre at Chipping Norton. Follow the B4450, in the direction of Stow, past the Town Hall and the Fox Hotel. At the Kings Arms turn left then right onto the Burford Road (A361) until the Chipping Norton School is reached, then go left at the hill top. Pass in front of the school buildings and follow the track straight ahead as indicated by the footpath sign.

2. At Glyme Farm turn right down the track for about 3yds, cross the stile, walk straight ahead passing the metal barns (left) to cross the stile in the wooden fence (right). Walk diagonally right to the bottom corner of the field, cross into the next field then go over the ditch-like River Glyme by the footbridge. Cross a further stile then go through the hedge where the path

is indicated by a yellow arrow marker.

3. Cross the next field bearing slightly right between the young trees, then continue over the fields by way of the stiles in the wire fences until, after passing the ruins of a farm building, you exit through a gateway onto a track with the river close by (right). Turn right and follow the track round a bend then at the junction fork right up the hill.

4. Soon the right of way becomes a pathway between high hedges and gradually climbs uphill for about 3/4 mile when it suddenly opens out into a wide gravel track. Pass through the metal gate (left) and descend the track towards Old Chalford Farm. Follow the track around (left) then (right) between the buildings as indicated by the blue arrow markers.

5. Pass through a gate and down the slope but before reaching the river turn left through a metal gate and walk along the grassy track by the river for about 1/2 mile to reach, via a wooden gate, the bend in the track we passed earlier. Turn right, continue up the hill passing New Chalford

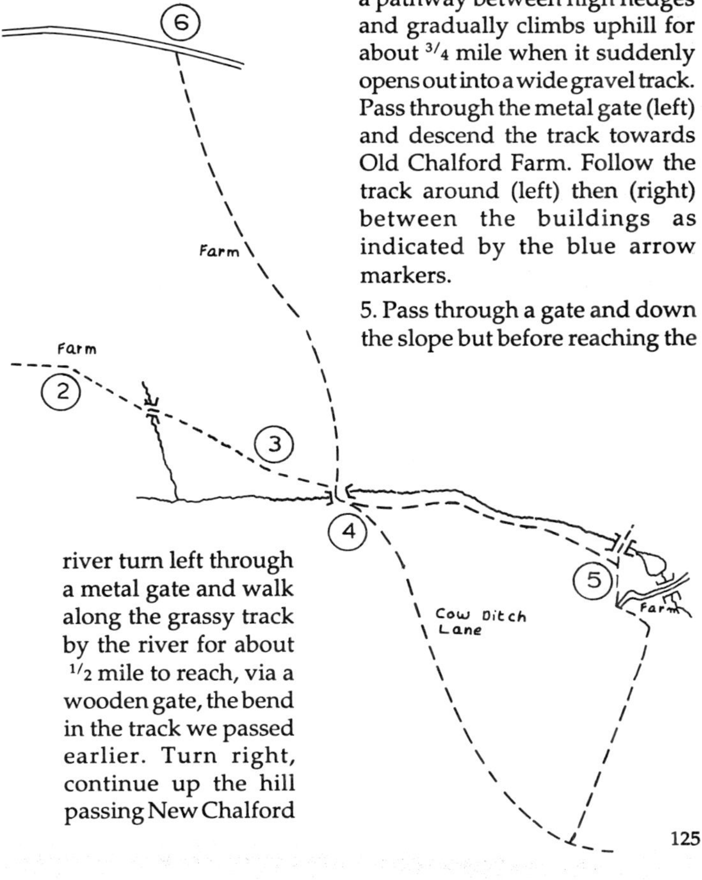

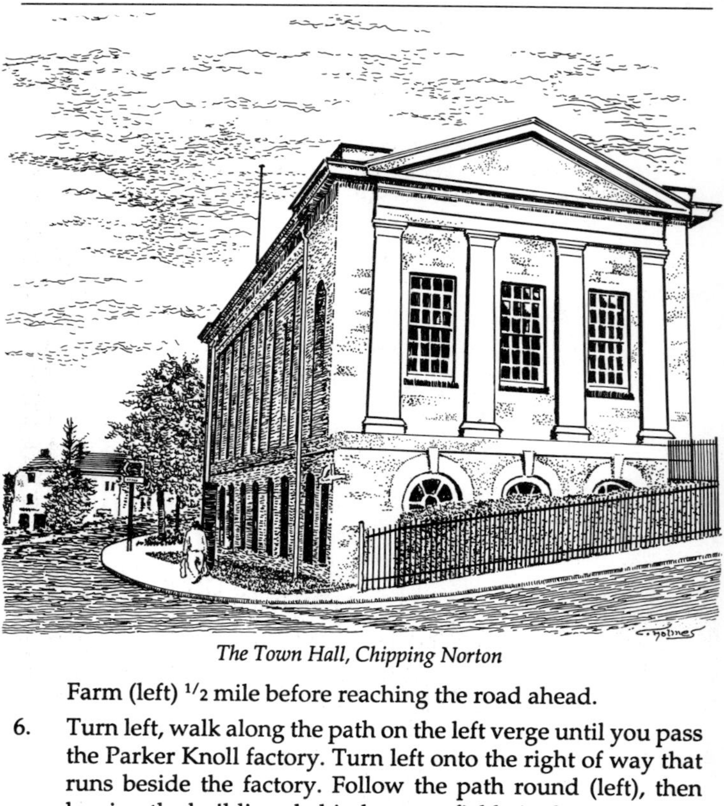

The Town Hall, Chipping Norton

Farm (left) $^{1}/_{2}$ mile before reaching the road ahead.

6. Turn left, walk along the path on the left verge until you pass the Parker Knoll factory. Turn left onto the right of way that runs beside the factory. Follow the path round (left), then leaving the buildings behind enter a field. At the gateway in the stone wall turn right and walk ahead towards the metal buildings and the water tower.

7. Pass between the farm buildings, follow the track round (right) then continue along the track until the road is reached. Turn left and at the Red Lion turn right into Cattle Market. At the bottom go right to the town centre.

St Mary's Church, Chipping Norton

Places and Points of Interest Along the Way

CHIPPING NORTON

Chipping Norton is the highest town in Oxfordshire. It has an attractive wide High Street which joins the market place where, in times gone by, horse fairs and markets were held. About the town centre there still remain shops and inns whose foundations were laid down over the last 300 years and while the Town Hall is a modern nineteenth-century building, the Guildhall at the opposite end of the market place dates from the sixteenth century.

From the High Street an attractive row of almhouses, dating from 1640, lead up to the Church of St Mary which was much rebuilt about 1485 by John Ashworth, the local wool merchant. Here, in the southern aisle, is a strikingly decorated window which fills the entire east end of the aisle; this, it is thought, came originally from the not too distant Bruern Abbey. Perhaps the most unusual feature of this church is its porch, which is hexagonal in shape and has a series of grinning devils carved onto the bosses inside.

Just to the north of the church is an area of irregular ground, alas this is all that remains of the Norman motte and bailey castle at Chipping Norton. To the west of the town stands a handsome former tweed mill. Known as the Bliss Valley Mill, it has a large domed tower and it was intended by its designer, the Lancashire mill architect George Woodhouse, that it should look like a large country house. He was certainly very successful in this aim for since his original design of 1872 the mill was operational until 1980 when it was converted into flats.

Stone devils decorate the inside of the porch of St Mary's

OLD CHALFORD AND THE RIVER SETTLEMENTS

Today the farm is virtually all that is left of the settlement that long ago stood here, its inhabitants working the land along the upper reaches of the River Glyme. About a mile down river is the tiny hamlet of Lidstone, consisting of a scattering of cottages and farm buildings. Midway between Lidstone and Old Chalford are a series of mounds and hollows - all that remains today of the former farming community at Nether Chalford. Here, at the time of

Domesday, was a thriving village but one which probably suffered so badly during the Black Death that it became depopulated.

Interestingly enough, part of the higher paths used on this walk are on what was in years gone by the old road linking Chipping Norton in the north with Oxford in the south, called Cow Ditch Lane.

The Almshouses, Chipping Norton

18: Adlestrop, Chastleton

Map Landranger:	163
Start:	GR: SP 242 269
Distance:	$3^{1}/_{2}$ miles

The route links the two small hamlets of Adlestrop and Chastleton. Starting over flat fields and farmland it gradually climbs a little as Chastleton is neared. The return, along a high track across Adlestrop hill, provides excellent views over the surrounding countryside. There are several sections, particularly in the wooded areas, that become very muddy in wet weather.

Route

1. So accommodating are the villagers of Adlestrop that they allow walkers to park their cars in the Village Hall car park. The only condition is that you close the gate after you. Leave the car park and turn left up the track. After crossing the wooden stile fork left, aim for the tree at the left corner of the field and right is Fenn Farm. Cross the stile, turn right then walk straight ahead past an oak tree and small barn (right) with ruined farm buildings over to the left.
2. Walk straight ahead climbing slightly to reach the stile with a yellow arrow marker. Go down the track, exit into a field then continue ahead up the field to a metal gate.
3. Turn right and follow blue arrows (left) through Peaswell Wood to the roadway. Chastleton is about $^{1}/_{2}$ mile distant (left), should you wish to visit.
4. To continue the walk, take the track sharp right from where you reached the roadway following it over Adlestrop Hill, where a seat is provided at the view point (right). Continue, passing the woods (left) to follow the track round (right) until a stile with a marker is reached (left), cross it and walk straight ahead through the woods to the road ahead.

5. Turn right at the road, follow it round (left) descend the hill taking the first turn left, with a bungalow (right) go down the lane following it round (right) to the road junction and with the church (left) walk ahead to return to the Village Hall.

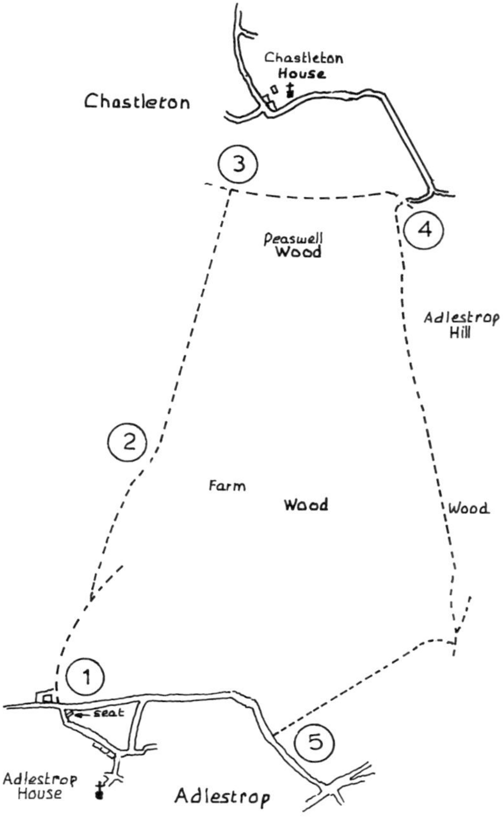

The Old Post Office and thatched cottages, Adlestrop

Places and Points of Interest Along the Way

ADLESTROP

The village station has long since gone as it was just one of so many local railway systems to suffer from the Beeching axe some years ago. Since there is little else at Adlestrop of any great significance, other than the Church of St Mary Magdalene, which was rebuilt in 1765 and the nearby rather grand Adlestrop Park, there would be little to tell except for the work of a Welsh poet.

The man who is responsible for putting Adlestrop on the map was Edward Thomas, a great lover of nature. He was born in 1878 and wrote profusely, before, like so many other talented and educated young men of his generation, he lost his life in the butchery of World War I. He was in fact only thirty-nine years old when he was killed at Arras. The Adlestrop poem was written by him following a rail journey he made from Battersea to Leddington via Chipping Campden during which an unscheduled stop was made at Adlestrop. His diary records the journey taking place on 23rd June 1914, the poem being written on 8th January the following year.

Since the station is no more, the station name of Adlestrop rests in the village bus shelter for all to see and on a plaque, on the seat,

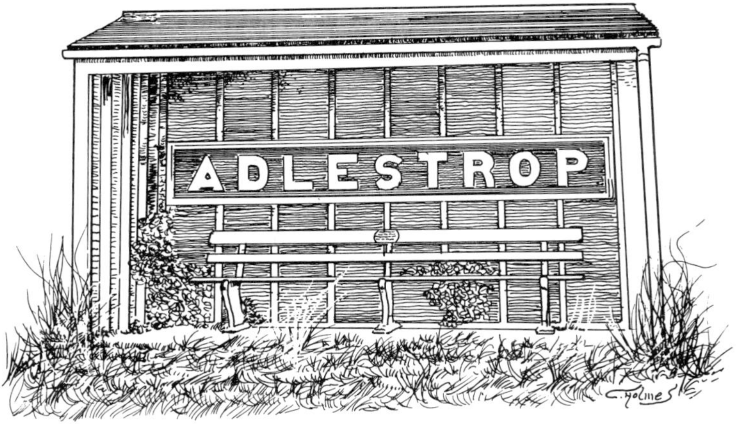

The Adlestrop poem is on the backrest of the seat

is engraved his poem:

Yes, I remember Adlestrop
The name, because one afternoon
Of heat the express-train drew up there
Unwontedly. It was late June.

The steam hissed. Someone cleared his throat.
No one left and no one came
On the bare platform. What I saw
Was Adlestrop - only the name.

And willows, willow-herb, and grass,
And meadowsweet, and haycocks dry,
No whit less still and lonely fair
Than the high cloudlets in the sky.

And for that minute a blackbird sang
Close by, and round his, mistier,
Farther and farther, all the birds
Of Oxfordshire and Gloucestershire.

The tiny hamlet has other literary connections. Jane Austen was one of them as her mother was first cousin to the Rev Thomas Leigh, one time rector of the parish. When Jane was nineteen she made her first visit to her relations, the Leighs, who lived at the manor, now

Chastleton House

Adlestrop Park, which the family had owned since the time of Elizabeth I. Jane was, it seemed, a self-proclaimed walking enthusiast and it is quite likely that she walked many of the local lanes, no doubt seeking inspiration for later works. It is probable that neighbouring Daylesford, the ancestral seat of Warren Hastings, was one of her favourite walks, for Hastings was to be a great admirer of her work.

The present village Church of St Mary Magdalene at Adlestrop is quite modern by Cotswold standards and in the main dates from the eighteenth century, the exceptions being the thirteenth-century chancel arch and the tower at the west end which dates from the fourteenth and fifteenth centuries.

CHASTLETON HOUSE

The Chastleton estate was at one point owned by Robert Catesby who, as most people will remember from their school days, was one of the members of the gunpowder plot conspiracy. He eventually sold the Chastleton estate for £4,000 to Walter Jones, a wealthy wool stapler, in order to raise money to pay for his part in the Essex rebellion.

The Jacobean house which has stood on this estate since it was built by Walter Jones around 1603 is a most imposing building which has undergone no major alterations since its original construction.

In 1651 during the Battle of Worcester, Arthur Jones, a relative of the original Walter Jones, took refuge in the house whilst fleeing from pursuers who mistook him for the King. According to one story his pursuers, failing to find him, spent the night in the very room behind the panels of which their quarry was hiding. Fortunately for Arthur Jones though, his wife Sarah drugged the Cromwellians with laudanum whilst her husband made good his escape.

During 1991 Chastleton House, regarded by many as one of the most notable of Britain's country houses of its period, was put on the market for the first time since it was sold by Robert Catesby. It is now owned by the National Trust, but closed for refurbishment until June 1996 when it will be open four days a week to limited numbers of visitors who will have to book in advance. The fabric of the house has been neglected for hundreds of years and large numbers of visitors will not be encouraged.

19: Stow-on-the-Wold, Broadwell

Map Landranger:	163
Start:	GR: SP 196 256
Distance:	3³/₄ miles

This short walk is ideal for a winter's day as it uses tarmac and gravel surfaces and is, for the most part, well sheltered. After passing through the old market town of Stow-on-the-Wold, the route takes in the small village of Broadwell with its pleasant pub, the Fox Inn.

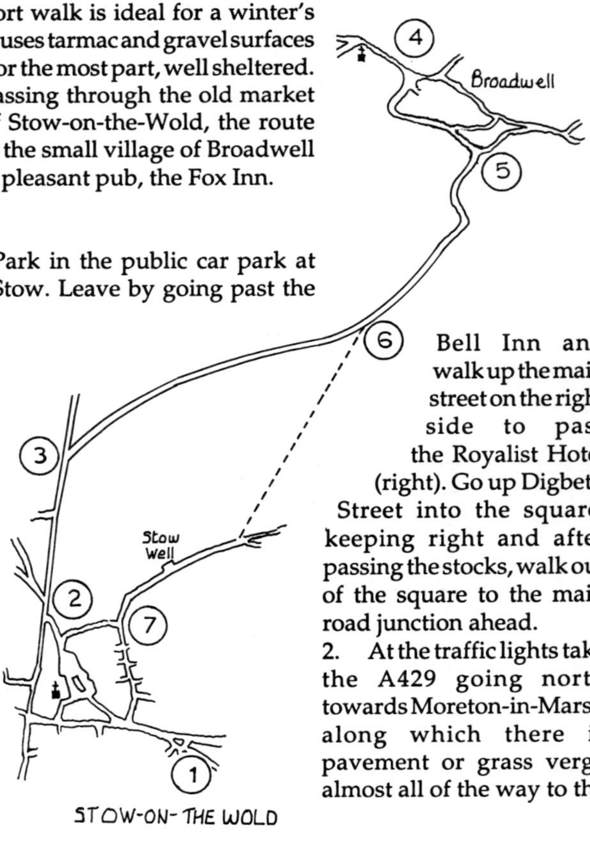

Route

1. Park in the public car park at Stow. Leave by going past the Bell Inn and walk up the main street on the right side to pass the Royalist Hotel (right). Go up Digbeth Street into the square, keeping right and after passing the stocks, walk out of the square to the main road junction ahead.

2. At the traffic lights take the A429 going north towards Moreton-in-Marsh along which there is pavement or grass verge almost all of the way to the

next junction (right), although you may wish to cross to the opposite side of the road at one point.

3. Turn right at the next road junction and follow the road down to the village of Broadwell. Turn left at the green, walk along the road passing the Fox Inn (left) and shortly after take the footpath to the church.

4. The pathway goes left of the church and joins the roadway at a junction. Turn right at the road and right again then follow it for about 3/8 of a mile to return to the village, passing the school (left) en-route.

5. The road directly opposite the ford, across the green, is the

Digbeth Street, Stow-on-the-Wold

The Square at Stow-on-the-Wold

road to Stow. Follow this, go around to the left then right up the hill; after a straight stretch of about 1/4 mile, turn left onto a bridleway.

6. After passing the cottage (left), the path turns right shortly after which Stow Well is passed right.
7. As you return to Stow, pass Glebe Close (right) and continue straight ahead until the end of Well Lane is reached. With the

The Fox Inn, Broadwell

Royalist Hotel now right, turn left, cross the road and go down the hill, entering the car park again, right of the Bell Inn.

Places and Points of Interest Along the Way

BROADWELL

This tiny village consists of a sprinkling of cottages and farm buildings set in a traditional manner around an enormous village green. It is quite an attractive little place, with the village hostelry, The Fox Inn, at one end, just across from the green, beyond which is the ford. The Church of St Paul's is a short distance away from the village and in the spring its attractiveness is enhanced by the colour from surrounding wild flowers. The church itself was founded during the twelfth century, although most of it dates from the late 1800s. Outside in the churchyard are a number of interesting tabletop tombs.

20: *Stow-on-the-Wold, Hyde Mill, Maugersbury*

Map Landranger:	163
Start:	GR: SP 196 256
Distance:	$3^{1}/_{2}$ miles

This route, a short stroll rather than a walk is a delightful way to spend a winter afternoon. After leaving the Fosse Way, the walker descends towards Hyde Mill across fields and through woods with fine views of Lower Swell down on the right. The return is through the quiet village of Maugersbury.

Route

1. At Stow-on-the-Wold park in the free car park just past the Bell Inn at the bottom of Park Street. Exit at the top of the car park and walk up the left side of Park Street which soon becomes Sheep Street. At the top of the hill turn left at the

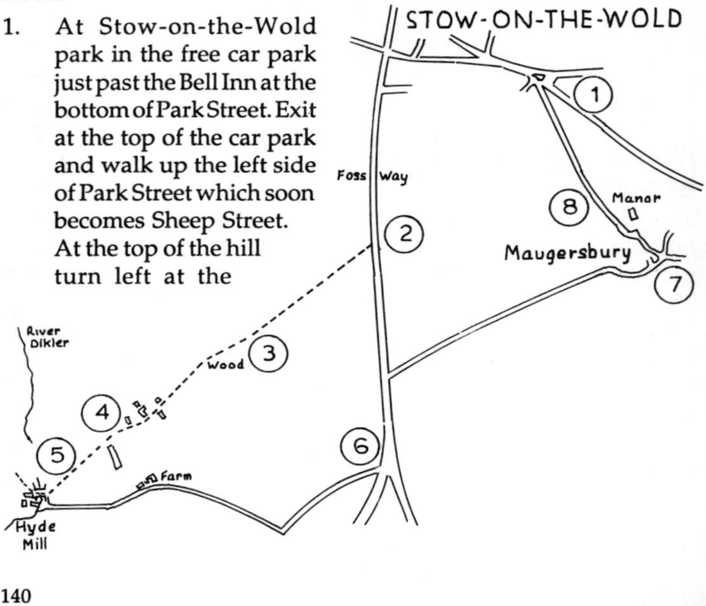

Hyde Mill

traffic lights onto the Fosse Way (A429). Staying on the left of this busy main road, walk down the hill until you have passed the Stow-on-the-Wold sign.

2. Cross the road, look for the sign and take the footpath to Lower Slaughter until you pass through the metal gate.

3. Cross the stile at the end of the track and pass into a field, then bear slightly right to pass through another gate and into the wood. Follow the path down through the trees exiting at an equestrian centre. Continue down the hill, pass through the double white gates (ahead) and walk between the buildings. The path diverts to the left to go round the last building on the right.
4. Just ahead on the telegraph pole, near a stile, is a yellow marker; go over the stile and into the field crossing to the bottom left hand corner to go through a wooden gate.
5. At Hyde Mill, turn left and continue along the bridleway passing farm buildings and cottages until you reach the busy main road junction (A429 to Cirencester).
6. Turn left and cross the road, climbing up the hill a short way in the direction of Stow. After the road direction sign, turn right into a disused road with an equestrian centre on the right. Continue through an avenue of trees following the lane to the village of Maugersbury.
7. As you enter the village, turn left where a road goes down to the right. Turn left through a large, rather grand pillared gateway, walk between the cottages and the old farm buildings to pass Maugersbury Manor on the right.
8. Continue along the track which soon becomes a wide tree-lined avenue until you return to the car park at Stow.

Places and Points of Interest Along the Way

STOW-ON-THE-WOLD

Stow is one of the most pleasant and popular of the Cotswolds towns, and at 700ft above sea level it is also the highest. The Abbot of Evesham named it Stow St Edward, the name it retained until the sixteenth century, when it became known as Stow-on-the-Wold. Busy all year round with a steady flow of visitors, Stow has been an important market town since medieval times. It has always been a traditional centre for sheep and horse fairs and at its height was reputed, by Daniel Defoe, to have seen the sale of 20,000 animals a day taking place. Even today a horse fair is still held twice a year.

At its centre is the large, almost triangular-shaped square

surrounded by buildings, many of which are of architectural interest. The Talbot Hotel, dating back to 1714, was formerly the Corn Exchange where samples of corn were brought for valuation. The existing letter box in the hotel wall is thought to be the place through which the corn samples were posted. To the left of the hotel is a narrow alley. A number of these alleys give access to the square and it is thought that they were designed so that the animals, primarily sheep, could be counted as they entered the sale area. Moving further round the square, is a lob-sided building, dating from 1450, which seems to defy all the rules of perspective. On the other side of the square are various inns and former staging posts. The Ross House was formerly known as The Plough and Charles I is said to have stayed at The Kings Arms at about the time of the Battle of Naseby. St Edwards Hall which dominates the square is quite modern by comparison, being built for a cost of £4,000 in 1878. The sum was provided from unclaimed deposits in the Town Savings Bank.

The cross in the Market Square was erected as a symbolic reminder to medieval market traders to deal honestly in the market place and to carry out their business transactions in a Christian manner. The cross was erected in the twelfth century and the headstone was added in 1878. Just off the square stands the Church of St Edward. When a large army of Royalists were defeated at Donnington in 1646 a thousand prisoners, the remainder of Sir Jacob Astley's army, were imprisoned in the church. In the aisle of St Edward's is the tomb of Captain Keyte, one of the Royalists, who died in the heavy fighting at Stow when the "gutters ran red with the blood of Englishmen fighting Englishmen". After the Civil War the church was declared a ruin until restoration work was carried out in 1700. Further restoration was carried out 200 years later. The tall tower is fifteenth century and in the west end of the church the Tudor stone mullioned window depicts Henry VII and his Queen.

Away from the square there are several more old inns - the eighteenth-century Queens Head, The Red Lion and the seventeenth-century White Hart. The Royalist Hotel, in Digbeth Street, has parts dating from around AD 947 and during the thirteenth to fifteenth centuries it was known as The Eagle and Child. During part of its varied history it also served as a hospice providing accommodation for the sick and the poor of the area. A letter written by the unfortunate Captain Keyte, the Commander of the Royalist Forces, was found here during restoration work and rumour has it that an underground passage connects with the Manor House at Maugersbury.

The stocks at Stow have been replaced regularly since the 1500s and the existing stocks were moved to their present position during the 1870s.

The stocks at Stow-on-the-Wold

Printed by CARNMOR PRINT & DESIGN,
95-97 LONDON ROAD, PRESTON, LANCASHIRE, UK.